Better Homes and Gardens®

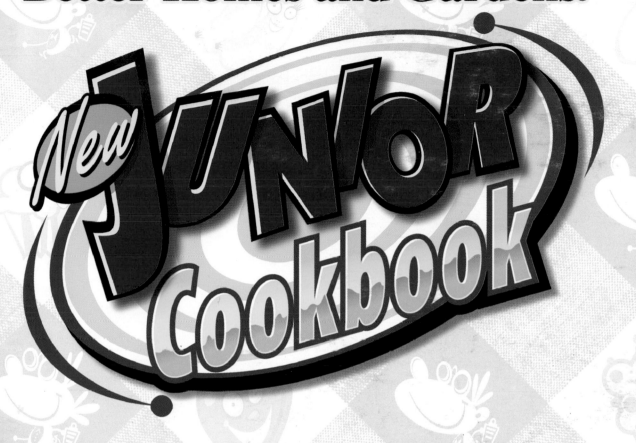

New JUNIOR Cookbook

Better Homes and Gardens® Books
Des Moines, Iowa

Better Homes and Gardens® Books
An imprint of Meredith® Books

New Junior Cookbook
Editor: Jennifer Dorland Darling
Contributing Editors: Maureen Fischer, Marty Schiel, Joyce Trollope
Design and Illustration: Wayne Vincent & Associates
Copy Chief: Angela K. Renkoski
Copy Editor: Jennifer Speer Ramundt
Proofreader: Susan Kling
Test Kitchen Director: Sharon Stilwell
Test Kitchen Home Economists: Marilyn Cornelius, product supervisor; Patricia Beebout, Jill Hoefler, Maryellyn Krantz, Debbie Parenza, Kay Springer, Colleen Weeden, Lori Wilson. Assistants: Barb Allen, Robbin Flanders, Jan Ross
Photographer: Jim Krantz
Food Stylist: Dianna Nolin
Editorial and Design Assistants: Judy Bailey, Jennifer Norris, Karen Schirm
Electronic Production Coordinator: Paula Forest
Production Director: Douglas M. Johnston
Production Manager: Pam Kvitne
Prepress Coordinator: Marjorie J. Schenkelberg

Meredith® Books
Editor in Chief: James D. Blume
Design Director: Matt Strelecki
Managing Editor: Gregory H. Kayko
Executive Food Editor: Lisa Holderness

Vice President, General Manager: Jamie L. Martin

Better Homes and Gardens® Magazine
Editor in Chief: Jean LemMon
Executive Food Editor: Nancy Byal

Meredith® Publishing Group
President, Publishing Group: Christopher M. Little
Vice President and Publishing Director: John P. Loughlin

Meredith® Corporation
Chairman of the Board: Jack D. Rehm
President and Chief Executive Officer: William T. Kerr
Chairman of the Executive Committee: E.T. Meredith III

All of us at Better Homes and Gardens® Books are dedicated to providing you with the information and ideas you need to create delicious foods. We welcome your comments and suggestions. Write to us at: Better Homes and Gardens Books, Cookbook Editorial Department, RW–240, 1716 Locust St., Des Moines, IA 50309–3023.

Our seal assures you that every recipe in the *New Junior Cookbook* has been tested in the Better Homes and Gardens® Test Kitchen. This means that each recipe is practical and reliable, and meets our high standards of taste appeal. We guarantee your satisfaction with this book for as long as you own it.

The recipe for Glob, page 108, is reprinted by permission of Marlor Press from *Kid's Squish Book*, by Loris Theovin Bree and Marlin Bree.

Contents

Start With the Basics, 4

It's Breakfast Time, 18

Let's Make Lunch, 32

I Need a Snack, 46

DINNER Is Served, 58

I'm Ready for Dessert, 80

Let's Celebrate, 92

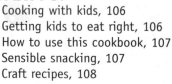

Calling All PARENTS, 104

Start with the BASICS

COME EXPLORE THE WORLD OF FOOD.

Learning to cook is an adventure that lasts a lifetime, one full of new flavor experiences, no two of which are exactly alike.

This cookbook will guide you on your exploration, teaching you how to read recipes and food labels, practice good kitchen safety, measure ingredients correctly, plan a menu, eat well, and even set a table. There's also a word list on pages 14 and 15 that defines some of the cooking terms used in these recipes.

Get started cooking today. Learning has never tasted so good.

READING RECIPES SUCCESSFULLY

The secret to being a successful cook is preparation.

● Begin by reading your chosen recipe from start to finish. Make sure you understand exactly what you're supposed to do. If you can't figure out a step and can't find the answer in this book, ask an adult to explain it to you.

● Make sure you have all the ingredients. If you don't, make a list of what you need. Ask an adult to help you buy them.

● Gather all the necessary equipment.

● Measure the ingredients accurately (see "Measuring basics" on this page).

● In general, it's a good idea to finish one recipe step before you start another.

● Practice good food-safety habits (see "Making safety the first ingredient," page 8, and "Keeping your food safe," page 9).

● When you're done, put away all the ingredients and equipment. Wash and dry the dirty dishes (or load them in the dishwasher). Wipe off the counters and table.

Measuring basics

The most basic rule in cooking is to measure accurately. You must use the right amount of each ingredient for a recipe to turn out well. To measure ingredients correctly, you'll need glass or clear-plastic measuring cups for liquid ingredients, metal or plastic measuring cups for dry ingredients, and measuring spoons.

Liquid ingredients

Glass measuring cups for liquids, such as milk, water, or juice, have lines marked on the glass to indicate the different amounts, and they have spouts to make pouring easy. Often these measurements will be in both cups and ounces.

To measure liquid ingredients, place a measuring cup on a flat surface. Add some of the liquid. Then bend down until your eyes are even with the measurement marks. If you don't have enough liquid, pour in a little more. Then check again. Do this until you have the right amount. If you have too much liquid, pour out the extra. Use a rubber scraper to make sure you get all the liquid out of the cup.

Use measuring spoons to measure small amounts of liquids. Hold the spoon away from the bowl or pan you're adding the liquid to, then pour enough liquid into the spoon to fill it.

Dry ingredients

Metal or plastic measuring cups are for dry ingredients such as flour, granulated sugar, nuts, shredded cheese, and bread crumbs. Each cup measures a different amount. Select the size the recipe calls for and spoon the ingredient into it. Using a narrow metal spatula, make the ingredient level with the top of the cup.

Measuring spoons for dry ingredients work in the same way.

If you don't have a measuring cup or spoon in the size specified, use smaller ones that together equal the amount needed. For example, if you don't have a ⅔-cup size, measure ⅓ cup of the ingredient. Pour the ingredient into the bowl or pan and measure another ⅓ cup. If you need ¾ cup, measure ½ cup and ¼ cup.

How do I measure...

Brown sugar

Brown sugar must be measured differently from other sugars because it clumps up. Use your fingers to pack the brown sugar into a dry measuring cup. Press down firmly. Add brown sugar until it is level with the top of the measuring cup. If done correctly, when you dump out the brown sugar, it will hold the shape of the cup.

Margarine or butter

One stick of margarine or butter equals ½ cup. To use smaller amounts, look for measurement marks on the wrapper. The marks indicate tablespoons, ¼ cup, and ⅓ cup. Use a table knife to cut the wrapped stick of margarine or butter at the mark you need. Unwrap the part you will use. Wrap the remainder in clear plastic wrap.

Shortening and peanut butter

Use a rubber scraper to pack shortening or peanut butter into a metal or plastic measuring cup. Cut through the shortening with the rubber scraper to squeeze out all the air. When the measuring cup is full, level off the top with the flat edge of the rubber scraper or a narrow metal spatula.
To remove the shortening or peanut butter from the measuring cup, run the rubber scraper around the inside of the cup and push the ingredient out. Be sure to scrape everything out of the cup.

Making safety the first ingredient

Too many cooks may spoil the broth, but when you're learning to cook, it's a good idea to have an adult along to help you. Ask your adult helper to read through the recipe with you and answer any questions you may have.

Make sure your adult helper shows you how to use all the equipment, particularly knives and electric appliances, such as a stove, oven, can opener, blender, food processor, and mixer. They can be tricky to use, so be sure your adult helper is standing by.

The best cooks are safe cooks. The following tips will help you cook safely.

● Wash your hands with lots of soap and water before you start. Keep your hands dry while cooking so you can have a good grip on your utensils.

● Wear an apron to keep your clothes clean. Don't wear shirts with long, loose sleeves. If your hair is long, tie it back.

● Keep a damp cloth or paper towel nearby to wipe up spills. Wiping up spills when they happen prevents accidents.

● Know where the first aid kit is. If you touch something hot, immediately hold your hand under cold water.

● Always use hot pads to handle hot items. Remember, anything you take from the oven, microwave oven, or stove will be hot and will stay hot for a while.

● Never set hot pots and pans directly on the counter. Always place a hot pad or wire cooling rack underneath a hot pot or pan.

● Tip lids open on casserole dishes and saucepans from the side farthest from you first. This allows the steam to escape away from you and not in your face. It's important to be careful because the steam can burn you.

● Turn saucepan and skillet handles to the middle of the stove. This way you won't bump a handle and spill hot food.

● Make sure mixers and blenders are turned off before you scrape the sides of the bowl. Have the mixer unplugged whenever you put in or take out the beaters.

● Use electric appliances away from water. If an appliance accidentally falls into the water while it's plugged in, DON'T TOUCH IT! Never plug in or unplug an electric appliance when your hands are wet.

● Use only microwave-safe equipment in the microwave oven. Aluminum foil containers, metal pans, and some glass or pottery dishes can cause sparks.

● Always pick up a knife or kitchen scissors by the handle. Leave all sharp items on the counter until you are ready to wash them. If you put them in a sink full of soapy water, you might reach in and accidentally cut yourself.

● Always keep the sharp edge of a knife pointed away from you and your hand when cutting food.

Keeping your food safe

Start clean and stay clean! That guideline applies to everything—hands, food, equipment, towels, and work surfaces. The following food-handling tips will make staying clean easier.

● Use a plastic cutting board to cut up raw poultry, meat, or fish. Wash the board with hot soapy water after every use and before using it with another type of food.

● Never put cooked poultry, fish, or meat on the same board or in the same container that held the raw meat, unless you have washed it well first.

● Wash fresh fruits and vegetables before eating or preparing them. Rinse poultry and pat dry with paper towels before cooking.

● Use only fresh foods. Spoiled foods can smell, look, and taste normal, but even a small bite could make you ill. If you're in doubt about its freshness, throw it out!

● Don't use cracked or dirty eggs. They may have been contaminated with harmful bacteria. Be sure to wash your hands, the equipment, and the countertop after working with eggs. Avoid eating raw eggs.

● Keep hot foods hot. Raw eggs, fish, poultry, and meat must be cooked well to kill harmful bacteria. If you have leftovers, put them into covered containers and refrigerate or freeze them as soon as possible.

● Keep cold foods cold. Foods that are meant to be refrigerated should be cold when you touch them. Frozen foods should be extremely cold and hard as a rock. Thaw foods in the refrigerator, not on the countertop.

Planning a menu

When you sit down in a restaurant, you are given a menu that describes all the food the restaurant can prepare. From that menu, you pick the dishes you want to eat. The chef who prepared that menu put a lot of thought into what to include. For instance, you'll probably see a selection of salads, vegetables, fish, poultry, meats, and desserts containing a range of necessary daily nutrients. There will be different flavors, colors, textures, and temperatures that appeal to many different tastes.

If you're the chef, it's up to you to decide what to serve. Here are a few tips to keep in mind when you're planning a menu:

● Include foods from the different food groups. Look at the Food Guide Pyramid on page 12 for ideas.

● Think about different colors, textures, and temperatures of foods. Mix crunchy foods with soft foods, hot foods with cold foods, and spicier foods with blander foods. Try to picture how the foods will look together on a plate and mix foods with a variety of colors and shapes.

● If one recipe is difficult or time consuming, pick simple recipes to round out the meal.

● Read all the recipes in your menu. Make sure each serves the number of people you're planning to serve. Then check to see what ingredients you need to purchase.

● Estimate how much time you will need to complete all of the preparation and cooking. Decide what time you want to eat. From those two figures you can determine what time you need to begin cooking.

● Prepare some of the recipes ahead of time, if you can. The less there is to do at the last minute, the better.

● Make a list of the recipes in your menu and anything else, such as bread or milk, that you'll be serving with the meal. Then check them off as you prepare them or put them on the table. It's a good way to double-check that you remembered everything.

Setting a table

A well-prepared meal deserves to be served on a well-set table. You'll need flatware (knives, forks, and spoons), glasses, plates, dishes, and napkins. If it's a special occasion, you might want to use place mats or a tablecloth.

Setting the table is as simple as one, two, three!

1. Count the number of people who will be eating. Then count out that number of knives, forks, spoons, glasses, plates, and napkins.

2. Set a plate, centered, in front of each chair. Put a fork to the left of each plate. Put a knife, blade edge pointing toward the plate, immediately to the right of each plate. Set a spoon just to the right of each knife.

3. Place a glass to the right of each plate above the knife. Set a napkin under each fork or to the left of each fork.

If you're going to serve several foods at one meal, you may need more dishes, flatware, and plates. Additional flatware should be added in the order in which it is to be used, with the items to be used first on the outside. For example, a salad fork goes to the left of the dinner fork. A salad plate goes directly to the left of the fork. A small bread-and-butter plate goes to the left of the dinner plate above the fork. A cup and saucer goes to the right of the glasses above the spoon.

When you pass dishes of food around the table, always pass to the right.

Eating well for healthy living

Since no one food contains all the nutrients you need, eating a little bit of everything is the best way to stay healthy.

It helps to think of foods in groups that form a pyramid when eaten in the proper amounts (see the Food Guide Pyramid, *top right*). The foods you should eat the most of to maintain good health—bread, cereal, rice, and pasta—are at the bottom of the Pyramid. The foods you should eat the least of—fats, oils, and sweets—are at the top.

If you follow the lessons of the Pyramid, you'll be eating lots of fruits, vegetables, and grains and getting lots of vitamins, such as vitamin C, which reduces your chances of getting a cold; minerals, such as calcium, which helps your teeth and bones grow strong; and fiber, which moves food through your body and gets rid of wastes.

Remember to drink lots of water, too. Because your body is more than half water, it is what keeps everything running smoothly.

The following list tells you how much you should eat from each group every day. (The number of servings are for kids; adults need more servings of bread, fruits, and vegetables.)

▶ **Bread, cereal, rice, and pasta**
You need to eat 6 to 9 servings every day. A serving could be 1 slice of bread; 1 ounce ready-to-eat cereal; or ½ cup cooked rice, cereal, or pasta.

▶ **Fruits**
You need 2 to 3 servings every day. A serving could be ½ cup cooked, canned, or frozen fruit; 4 tablespoons dried fruit; ¾ cup 100-percent fruit juice; or 1 medium apple, banana, orange, pear, or peach.

▶ **Vegetables**
You need 3 to 4 servings every day. A serving could be 1 cup of mixed greens, ½ cup raw or cooked vegetables, or ¾ cup vegetable juice.

▶ **Milk, yogurt, and cheese**
You need 2 to 3 servings every day. A serving could be 1 cup milk or yogurt, 1½ ounces natural cheese, or 2 ounces process cheese.

▶ **Meat, poultry, fish, dry beans, eggs, and nuts**
You need 2 to 3 servings every day. A serving could be 3 ounces cooked, lean, boneless meat, poultry, or fish or 2 to 3 equivalents of 1 ounce of meat (½ cup cooked dry beans; 2 tablespoons peanut butter; or 1 egg is equivalent to, or the same as, 1 ounce of meat).

▶ **Fats, oils, and sweets**
Try not to eat foods with lots of fat, oil, or sugar. These supply calories, but few, if any, vitamins and minerals.

Reading food labels

According to the law, most packaged foods must come with information about how good those foods are for you. There are two parts of the label you should learn to read: the Nutrition Facts and the ingredients list.

Look at the Nutrition Facts label on a food item you have at home. It will tell you:

- How much one serving is
- How many servings are in the package
- How many calories are in one serving
- How much protein, carbohydrate, fat, and saturated fat are in one serving (these are in the metric unit "grams," shown as "g")
- How much sodium and cholesterol are in one serving (these are in the metric unit "milligrams," shown as "mg")
- What recommended Daily Values of the nutrients are in the food (the percentage of the total amount of that nutrient in one serving that you need every day). To see if you have reached the recommended Daily Value of a nutrient, think in terms of points. You start each day needing 100 points for each of the nutrients on the label. For instance, if the Daily Value for sodium in a product is 25 percentage points, subtract 25 from 100; you're left needing 75 more percentage points of sodium. In other words, you've had 25 percent, or one-fourth, of what you need after you've eaten one serving of that food.

The ingredients list tells you what has been used to make the food product. Because packaged foods often contain more than one ingredient, the ingredients are listed on the label starting with the one that, according to weight, makes up most of that food. For instance, if sugar is listed first on a package of cookies, it means that the cookies contain more sugar than any other ingredient.

What's up with Nutrition Facts

Every recipe in this book includes nutrition information. You'll find it at the top of the page. Our Test Kitchen uses a computer analysis of each recipe to determine the nutritional value of a single serving. Here's how it works:

- We use the first serving size when a range is given. For example, if a recipe is said to make 4 to 6 servings, we analyze the nutrition based on four servings.
- When ingredient choices appear in a recipe (such as margarine or butter), we use the first one mentioned for analysis. The ingredient order does not mean we prefer one ingredient over another.
- When milk is an ingredient in a recipe, the analysis is calculated using 2-percent milk.
- The analysis does not include ingredients we say are optional in the recipe.

Talking like a cook

If you're a little bit puzzled by a word in a recipe, check this list for an explanation.

Bake. Cook food in the oven.

Beat. Beating is used to add air to a mixture and make it smooth. To beat by hand, mix the food with a fork or a wooden spoon in a fast up-and-down motion. You also can use a rotary beater or electric mixer.

Boil. Cook food on top of the stove over high heat so lots of big bubbles form quickly, then break at the surface.

Broil. Cook food by direct heat under a broiler in an electric or gas range.

Brown. Cook food until it starts to look brown on the outside.

Chill. Put food in the refrigerator to make it completely cold.

Chop. Use a sharp knife—ask an adult to help you—and a cutting board. First slice the food evenly, making all the pieces about the same thickness. Then cut the slices into lots of small pieces that are about the same size. They don't have to be the same shape, but they should be about the size of peas. You also can chop foods with an electric blender or food processor; again, ask an adult for help.

Combine. Mix ingredients together.

Cool. Let food stand on the counter until it is no longer hot. If you put the food on a wire cooling rack, it will cool more quickly and evenly because the air can move all around it.

Cover. Put plastic wrap, foil, waxed paper, or a bowl cover over a dish of food to keep the air out. It helps prevent food from spoiling.

Crack an egg. Tap an uncooked egg with a table knife around the middle until it starts to crack. Or, tap the egg on the side of a bowl. Working over a bowl, pull the eggshell halves apart and let the egg white and yolk fall into the bowl. If eggshell pieces fall into the bowl, lift them out with a spoon.

Dash. A dash of an ingredient is a small amount—much less than $\frac{1}{8}$ teaspoon. To add a dash of an ingredient, just sprinkle a little out into your palm. Then add it to the mixture.

Dissolve. Stir a dry ingredient (like sugar) into a liquid (like water) until it disappears.

Drain. Set food in a colander or sieve so the liquid separates from the solid portion.

Grate. Rub an ingredient across the smallest holes on a grater to break the ingredient into the smallest pieces possible.

Grease. Put some shortening, butter, or margarine, on a small piece of paper towel or waxed paper. Rub the shortening evenly on the inside of the pan. You also can use nonstick spray coating, which comes in a can. Greasing a pan keeps food from sticking to it. Sometimes a coating of flour also is necessary. Add a small amount of all-purpose flour to the pan after it is greased. Working over the sink, gently rotate and tap the pan until the greased area is coated with flour.

Knead. Working with the dough on the counter, use your hands to push against the dough. Then fold the dough, turn it, and push against it again to make it smooth.

Measure. Allot a specific amount of an ingredient (see "Measuring basics," pages 6 and 7).

Melt. Turn a solid into a liquid by heating it.

Menu. A list of food to be served at a meal. It should include something from each basic food group in the Food Guide Pyramid (see page 12 for the food groups and page 10 to plan a menu).

Mix. Stir ingredients together so the mixture looks the same all over.

Peel. Remove the outer skin from vegetables or fruits using a vegetable peeler (as with carrots and potatoes) or your hands (as with oranges and bananas).

Shred. Rub an ingredient across a shredder to make long, thin pieces. (Shredded cheese, for example, is what you put on a pizza.)

Simmer. Cook food on top of the stove over high heat until lots of small bubbles come to the surface and break gently. Then turn the burner to low. Cover the mixture with a lid, if it says to in the recipe.

Slice. Use a sharp knife (ask an adult to help you) and a cutting board. Holding the food firmly on the board, cut a thin piece off the end. Repeat until all the ingredient is cut into pieces of about the same thickness.

Stir-fry. Quickly cook food in a small amount of oil in a hot skillet or wok.

Toss. Mix ingredients lightly in a bowl by lifting them with two spoons, two forks, or your hands, then letting them fall back into the bowl.

Equipment

Baking sheet or
cookie sheet

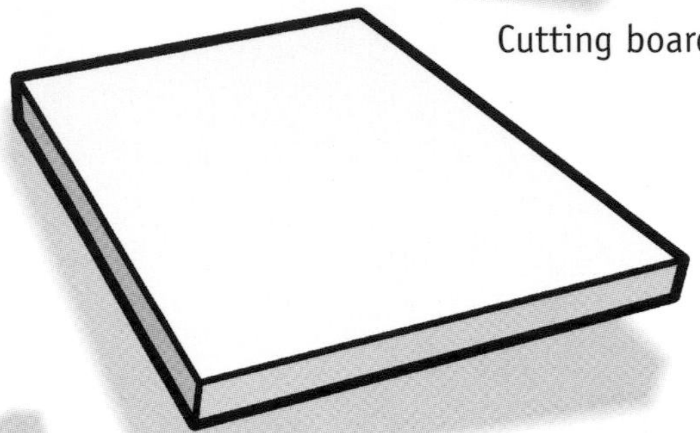

Cutting board

Colanders

Electric blender

Electric mixer

Juicer

Kitchen
scissors

Measuring cups

Measuring spoons

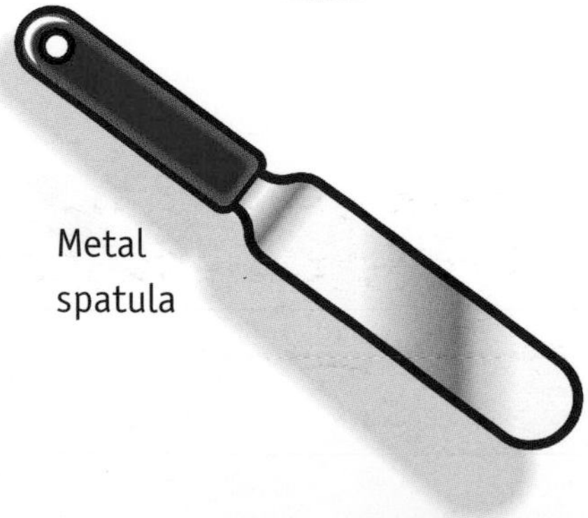

Metal
spatula

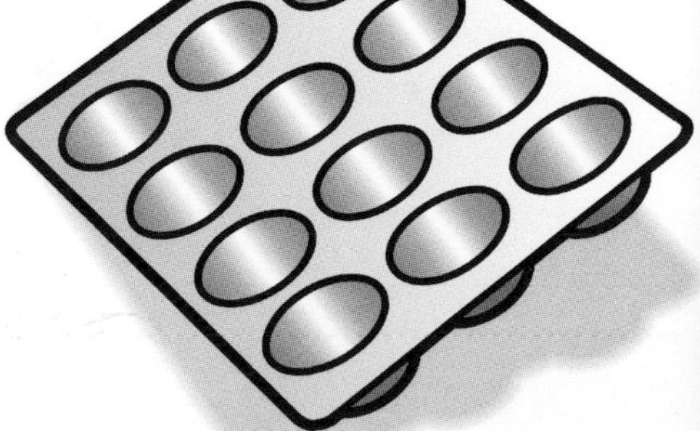

Muffin
pan

Pancake turner

Rotary beater

Rubber scraper

Saucepans

Sharp knife

Sieve

Skillet

Table knife

Slotted spoon

Wire cooling rack

Tongs

Vegetable peeler

Wire whisk

Wooden spoon

17

Prep: 20 minutes
Cook: 4 minutes each
Makes 8 to 10 standard-size (4-inch) pancakes.

FLAT AS A PANCAKE

Call them what you like: flapjacks, griddle cakes, hotcakes, flannel cakes, or just plain pancakes.

Ingredients

1 cup all-purpose flour
1 tablespoon granulated sugar
1 teaspoon baking powder
¼ teaspoon baking soda
¼ teaspoon salt
1 egg
1 cup buttermilk
2 tablespoons cooking oil
    Shortening
    Syrup or powdered sugar, if you like

Utensils

Griddle or large skillet
2 medium mixing bowls
Measuring cups
Measuring spoons
Wooden spoon
Fork
Pancake turner

Nutrition Facts Per Pancake

Calories	111
Total fat	5 g
Saturated fat	1 g
Cholesterol	28 mg
Sodium	192 mg
Carbohydrate	14 g
Fiber	0 g
Protein	3 g

Kid-testers Caitlyn and Elena preferred to make silly shapes with the pancake batter. You can, too, by spooning the batter into a sealable plastic bag. Snip off one corner and gently squeeze the batter onto the hot griddle in any shape you like.

1. Put flour, sugar, baking powder, baking soda, and salt in a mixing bowl. Stir with the wooden spoon to mix. Save until Step 3.

2. Crack egg into the other mixing bowl. Beat with the fork until yolk and white are mixed. Add buttermilk and oil to egg. Beat with the fork until ingredients are well mixed.

3. Add egg mixture to dry ingredients. Stir with the wooden spoon until dry ingredients are wet. (The batter should be somewhat lumpy, not smooth.)

4. Grease an unheated griddle or large skillet. Heat the griddle or skillet over medium heat until hot. (To check if the griddle or skillet is ready, sprinkle a few drops of water on the surface. The water will dance across the surface when the griddle is hot enough.)

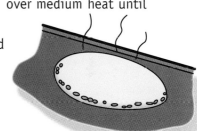

pancakes have bubbly surfaces and the edges are slightly dry. (This will take about 2 minutes.)

5. For each pancake, pour about ¼ cup batter onto the hot griddle or skillet. Cook over medium heat until

6. Turn the pancakes over with the pancake turner. Cook until bottoms are golden brown (about 2 minutes more). Turn off burner. Remove griddle or skillet from burner. Serve pancakes with syrup or powdered sugar, if you like.

Sauce It!

Make a simple blueberry sauce for the pancakes with ½ cup canned blueberry pie filling and 2 tablespoons orange juice. Stir them together in a small bowl and heat in a microwave oven for about 1 minute or until mixture is warm.

Serve with...
crisp bacon strips and apple juice and milk.

Riddle Griddle BREAD

Prep: 15 minutes
Cook: 3 minutes each
Makes 3 servings.

To us it's **"French toast,"** but French people call it "lost bread." Know why? Because they use leftover (or lost) French bread that's too dry to eat unless it's dipped in the eggs and milk.

Ingredients

2 eggs
½ cup milk
⅛ teaspoon ground cinnamon, if you like
2 tablespoons margarine or butter
6 slices firm-textured white bread*
Maple-flavored syrup

Utensils

Medium mixing bowl
Rotary beater or fork
Measuring cup
Measuring spoon
9-inch pie plate
Table knife
Large skillet
Pancake turner

Nutrition Facts Per Serving	
Calories	276
Total fat	13 g
Saturated fat	3 g
Cholesterol	145 mg
Sodium	456 mg
Carbohydrate	29 g
Fiber	0 g
Protein	10 g

1. Crack eggs into mixing bowl. Beat with rotary beater or fork until yolks and whites are mixed together. Add milk and cinnamon, if you like. Beat until ingredients are well mixed. Pour egg mixture into pie plate.

2. Put half of the margarine or butter in skillet. Put the skillet on a burner. Turn the burner to medium heat and let margarine melt.

3. Dip 1 slice of bread into egg mixture. Turn bread over with pancake turner to coat the other side. Put coated bread in skillet. Repeat with a second slice of bread.

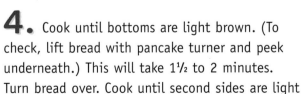

4. Cook until bottoms are light brown. (To check, lift bread with pancake turner and peek underneath.) This will take 1½ to 2 minutes. Turn bread over. Cook until second sides are light brown (about 1½ to 2 minutes more). Remove bread from the skillet.

5. If necessary, put remaining margarine or butter in skillet. Repeat steps 3 and 4 with remaining bread and egg mixture. Turn off burner. Remove skillet from burner. Serve French toast with maple-flavored syrup.

If you don't use firm-textured bread, such as French bread, cover bread slices with paper towels and let them stand out on a counter for several hours or until they are dry.

Serve with... fresh orange sections and milk.

Egg-ceptional
Breakfast Bake

Put all your eggs in one dish—along with ham and your favorite cheese, such as cheddar, Swiss, Monterey Jack with jalapeño, or American.

Ingredients

Shortening

6 slices bread

1 2½-ounce package very thinly sliced cooked ham

½ cup shredded cheddar cheese

6 eggs

1¼ cups milk

⅛ teaspoon pepper

Utensils

2-quart rectangular baking dish

Measuring cups

Measuring spoons

4-cup measuring cup or medium bowl

2-cup measuring cup

Table knives

Rotary beater or fork

Plastic wrap

Hot pads

Wire cooling rack

Nutrition Facts Per Serving

Calories	224
Total fat	11 g
Saturated fat	5 g
Cholesterol	233 mg
Sodium	439 mg
Carbohydrate	16 g
Fiber	0 g
Protein	5 g

Collin,
a kid-tester and experienced egg eater, suggests using cooked chicken or turkey in place of the ham.

1. Grease 2-quart rectangular baking dish with shortening. Tear bread into bite-size pieces. Sprinkle half of the bread pieces into the bottom of the baking dish.

2. Cut ham into bite-size pieces using a table knife (you should have about ½ cup). Sprinkle ham and cheese over bread in baking dish. Sprinkle remaining torn bread over ham and cheese.

3. Crack eggs into 4-cup measuring cup or medium bowl. Add milk and pepper to eggs. Mix with the rotary beater or fork until whites, yolks, and other ingredients are well mixed. Pour egg mixture over bread layers in the baking dish. Cover dish with plastic wrap.

4. Chill in the refrigerator at least 2 hours, but not more than 24 hours.

5. Turn on the oven to 325°. Remove plastic wrap from baking dish. Put dish in the oven. Bake for 35 minutes.

6. Use hot pads to pull out oven rack slightly. To see if food is cooked, stick a table knife into the center of the food in the dish. If the knife comes out clean, remove baking dish from oven. If it does not come out clean, bake 2 to 3 minutes longer and test again. Turn off oven. Place baking dish on the cooling rack and let cool 10 minutes. Cut into squares to serve.

Serve with...
bowls of sliced strawberries sprinkled with powdered sugar and glasses of milk.

MASTERPIECE MUFFINS

Prep: 25 minutes
Bake: 20 minutes
Makes 10 muffins.

Dress up the muffin tops by sprinkling on a crumbly streusel mixture.

Ingredients

Shortening
2 tablespoons all-purpose flour
2 tablespoons brown sugar
$1/8$ teaspoon ground cinnamon
1 tablespoon butter or margarine
$1^3/4$ cups all-purpose flour
$1/3$ cup granulated sugar
2 teaspoons baking powder
$1/4$ teaspoon salt
1 egg
$3/4$ cup milk
$1/4$ cup cooking oil

Utensils

Muffin pan with ten $2^1/2$-inch cups
2 medium mixing bowls
Wooden spoon
Pastry blender
Small mixing bowl
Measuring cups
Measuring spoons
Fork
Hot pads
Wire cooling rack

Nutrition Facts Per Muffin	
Calories	188
Total fat	8 g
Saturated fat	2 g
Cholesterol	26 mg
Sodium	154 mg
Carbohydrate	26 g
Fiber	1 g
Protein	3 g

1. Turn on the oven to 400°. Grease ten 2½-inch muffin pan cups with shortening. Save until Step 7.

2. For the streusel topping, put 2 tablespoons flour, 2 tablespoons brown sugar, and cinnamon in mixing bowl. Stir with wooden spoon to mix.

3. Use the pastry blender with a chopping motion to mix in butter or margarine until the mixture is crumbly. Save until Step 7.

4. Put 1¾ cups flour, the sugar, baking powder, and salt in the medium mixing bowl. Stir with the wooden spoon to mix. Save until Step 6.

5. Crack egg into the small mixing bowl. Beat with the fork until yolk and white are mixed together. Add milk and oil to egg. Beat with the fork until ingredients are well mixed.

6. Add egg mixture to dry ingredients. Stir with the wooden spoon until dry ingredients are wet. (The batter should be somewhat lumpy, not smooth.)

7. Spoon some of the batter into each muffin cup. Sprinkle 1 rounded teaspoon of the streusel topping over the top of each muffin cup of batter.

8. Put muffin pan in oven. Bake 20 minutes or until muffins are golden. Turn off oven.

9. Use hot pads to remove muffin pan from the oven. Tip muffin pan to carefully remove muffins onto the cooling rack. Cool muffins on cooling rack about 10 minutes.

Oatmeal UNREAL!

Bet you never thought oatmeal could be your berry favorite breakfast!

Ingredients

2 cups fresh raspberries or strawberries or frozen lightly sweetened red raspberries or unsweetened whole strawberries

2 tablespoons honey

3 cups water

1½ cups quick-cooking rolled oats

Utensils

Measuring cups
Measuring spoon
Medium mixing bowl
Wooden spoon
Potato masher ·················
Medium saucepan and lid
Large spoon
4 cereal bowls

Nutrition Facts Per Serving

Calories	179
Total fat	2 g
Saturated fat	0 g
Cholesterol	0 mg
Sodium	7 mg
Carbohydrate	36 g
Fiber	3 g
Protein	5 g

1. If you are using frozen raspberries or strawberries, thaw them according to the directions on the package.

2. Put fresh or thawed raspberries or strawberries and honey in the mixing bowl. Mash with a potato masher or stir with a wooden spoon to mix well and slightly crush the berries. Save until Step 4.

3. Put water and oats in the saucepan. Stir with a wooden spoon to mix. Put the pan on a burner. Turn the burner to medium-high heat. Cook just until bubbly, stirring all the time. Turn off burner. Remove saucepan from heat and cover. Let oatmeal stand for 5 minutes.

4. Use the large spoon to put the oatmeal into the cereal bowls. Spoon some of the raspberry or strawberry mixture into each bowl. Gently swirl berries into the oatmeal.

Serve with... buttered, toasted English muffins and milk.

29

Groovie SMOOTHIES

Sip, slurp, swallow, and burp— it's quick as a wink and a pretty cool drink!

Ingredients

2 ripe small bananas

1 cup frozen unsweetened whole strawberries

1 8-ounce carton vanilla low-fat yogurt

¾ cup milk

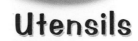

Utensils

Table knife

Measuring cups

Electric blender ·············

2 tall glasses

Rubber scraper ·············

Nutrition Facts Per Serving	
Calories	259
Total fat	5 g
Saturated fat	3 g
Cholesterol	13 mg
Sodium	113 mg
Carbohydrate	49 g
Fiber	3 g
Protein	9 g

1. Remove the peel from the bananas. Using the table knife, cut bananas into chunks.

2. Put banana chunks, frozen strawberries, yogurt, and milk into the blender container.

3. Cover blender with the lid and blend on high speed about 1 minute or until mixture is smooth. Turn off blender. Pour drink into 2 glasses. Use rubber scraper to get all of the drink out of the blender.

Serve with... pieces of toast spread with peanut butter or bowls of cereal with milk.

unch

Tom Thumb's Tacos

Start to finish:
25 minutes

Makes 24 mini tacos or
8 regular-size tacos
(4 to 6 servings).

Small in size, but these tacos pack a **GIANT** taste— especially if you use hot salsa.

Ingredients

12 ounces ground beef

1/2 cup salsa

1/2 teaspoon dried oregano, crushed

4 lettuce leaves

24 mini or 8 regular-size taco shells*

3/4 cup shredded cheddar cheese
(3 ounces)

Dairy sour cream, chopped tomato, and/or salsa, if you like

Utensils

Large skillet with lid

Wooden spoon

Colander

Hot pads

Medium bowl

Measuring cups

Measuring spoons

Spoon

Tongs

34

Nutrition Facts Per Serving

Calories	65
Total fat	4 g
Saturated fat	2 g
Cholesterol	13 mg
Sodium	65 mg
Carbohydrate	3 g
Fiber	0 g
Protein	4 g

Jacob and Jason proclaimed these "Delicious!" and said they'd try regular-size taco shells for bigger bites.

1. Put ground beef in the skillet; use the wooden spoon to break up meat. Put the skillet on a burner. Turn the burner to medium-high heat. Cook until no pink color is left in meat, stirring now and then with the wooden spoon. This will take 8 to 10 minutes. Turn off burner. Remove skillet from burner.

2. Place colander over bowl. Spoon meat into the colander and let the fat drain into the bowl. Spoon meat back into skillet. Put fat in a container to throw away.

3. Stir ½ cup salsa and the oregano into meat. Cover skillet and put skillet on a burner. Turn the burner to medium heat. Cook for 5 minutes, stirring with the wooden spoon after about 3 minutes. Turn off burner. Remove skillet from burner. Put meat in a bowl.

4. While meat mixture is cooking, tear or cut lettuce into bite-size pieces.

5. To make tacos, let each person spoon some of the meat mixture into each taco shell. Add lettuce and cheese. Top with sour cream, chopped tomato, and extra salsa, if you like.

If you like, make taco shells crisp by placing them on a baking sheet and warming them in a 350° oven for 5 to 7 minutes or until they are the desired crispness. Turn off oven. Use hot pads to remove baking sheet from oven. Use tongs to put shells on a cool plate.

Taco Salad: Use 2 cups of tortilla chips in place of the taco shells. Spoon other ingredients—meat mixture, lettuce, cheese, sour cream, tomato, and extra salsa—over the chips.

Serve with... carrot sticks, apple slices, and milk.

L
U
N
C
H

Totally AWESOME Tortillas

Start to finish:
25 minutes
Makes 4 servings.

They're **too cool** for rules, so you pick the filling—either the refried beans, below, or the taco meat mixture on page 35.

Ingredients

- 4 10-inch flour tortillas
- 1 16-ounce can refried beans or, if you like, one 15-ounce can black beans
- $\frac{1}{4}$ teaspoon ground cumin
- $\frac{1}{2}$ cup salsa or picante sauce
- $\frac{1}{2}$ cup shredded taco cheese or cheddar cheese (2 ounces)
- $\frac{1}{2}$ cup lettuce torn into small pieces

  Additional salsa or picante sauce, if you like

Utensils

Foil

Can opener

Colander, if you use black beans

Medium bowl, if you use black beans

Potato masher, if you use black beans

Medium saucepan

Wooden spoon

Hot pads

Measuring cups

Measuring spoons

Nutrition Facts Per Serving	
Calories	323
Total fat	10 g
Saturated fat	4 g
Cholesterol	15 mg
Sodium	860 mg
Carbohydrate	46 g
Fiber	6 g
Protein	14 g

Microwave directions

Place the tortillas between paper towels. Heat on 100% power (high) for 20 to 30 seconds or until softened and warm. (Warm the tortillas just before you're ready to fill them.)

1. Turn on the oven to 350°. Wrap tortillas in foil. Put wrapped tortillas in oven. Bake about 10 minutes or until tortillas are warm.

2. Open can of beans. (If you are using black beans, pour beans into a colander, rinse with cold water, and drain thoroughly. Put black beans into the bowl and mash them with the potato masher.) Put refried beans or mashed black beans into the saucepan. Stir cumin into beans. Put the saucepan on the burner. Turn the burner to medium heat. Cook about 5 minutes or until beans are warm, stirring now and then with the wooden spoon. Turn off burner. Remove saucepan from burner.

3. Turn off oven. Use hot pads to remove tortillas from oven.

4. Spoon about ¼ cup of the beans near one edge of each tortilla. Add 2 tablespoons salsa or picante sauce, 2 tablespoons cheese, and 2 tablespoons lettuce. Roll tortillas around filling. Serve with additional salsa or picante sauce, if you like.

Serve with...

celery sticks, cottage cheese with a pineapple slice, and milk.

Prep: 20 minutes
Bake: 8 minutes
Makes 4 servings.

Doubly Crusty Pizza

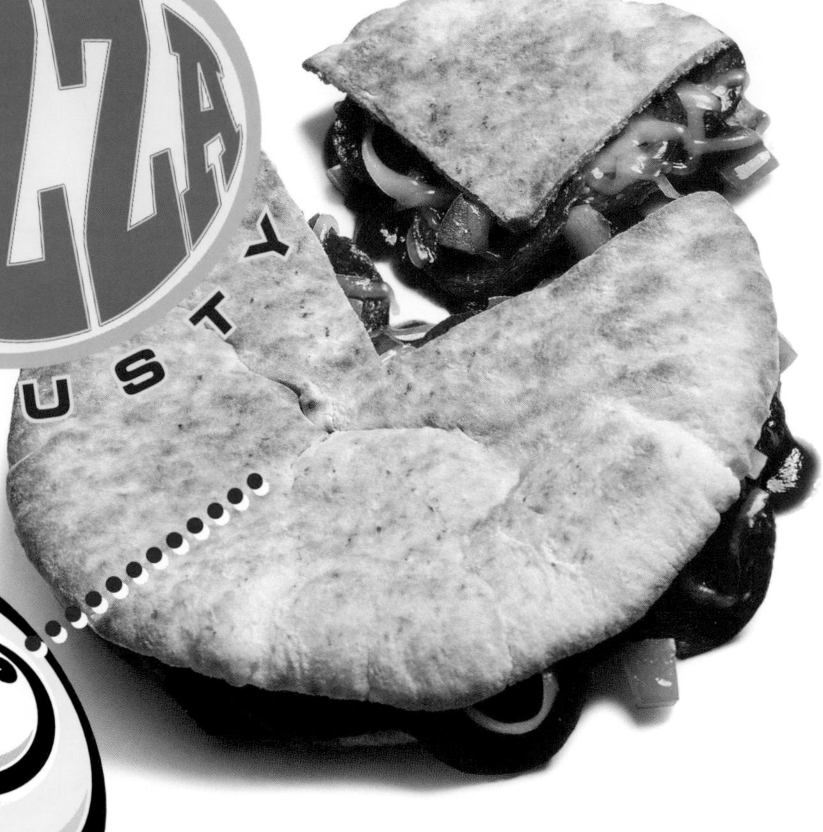

Don't tell anyone what's hidden under the top crust. Let the first bite be a surprise.

Utensils

- Baking sheet
- Foil
- Scissors
- Toaster
- Cutting board
- Sharp knife
- Measuring cups
- Can opener
- Hot pads
- Wire cooling rack
- Pizza cutter

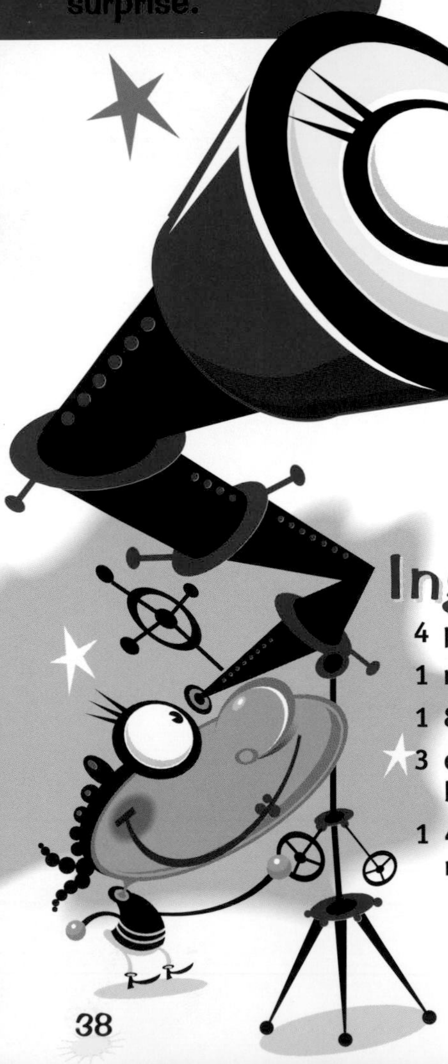

Ingredients

- 4 pita bread rounds (about 6 inches across)
- 1 medium green sweet pepper
- 1 8-ounce can pizza sauce
- 3 ounces sliced pepperoni or Canadian-style bacon
- 1 4-ounce package (1 cup) shredded mozzarella cheese

Nutrition Facts Per Serving	
Calories	383
Total fat	16 g
Saturated fat	6 g
Cholesterol	43 mg
Sodium	1,217 mg
Carbohydrate	43 g
Fiber	1 g
Protein	18 g

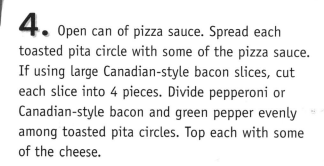

1. Cover the baking sheet with foil for easier cleanup. Turn on the oven to 400°. Using scissors, cut around the edge of each pita bread round, splitting each into 2 circles and making a total of 8 circles. Save 4 circles for Step 4.

2. Toast 4 pita circles in a toaster, one at a time. (If pita circles are too large for the toaster, place them on a baking sheet and bake in a 400° oven for 2 minutes.)

3. On the cutting board use the sharp knife to cut green pepper in half from top to bottom. Pull off stem and throw away. Remove seeds and soft white parts from inside the pepper halves and throw away. Cut pepper halves into small pieces (you should have about ¾ cup).

4. Open can of pizza sauce. Spread each toasted pita circle with some of the pizza sauce. If using large Canadian-style bacon slices, cut each slice into 4 pieces. Divide pepperoni or Canadian-style bacon and green pepper evenly among toasted pita circles. Top each with some of the cheese.

5. Place untoasted pita circles on top. Place on baking sheet. Put baking sheet in the oven. Bake 8 to 10 minutes or until hot and cheese has melted. Turn off oven. Use hot pads to remove baking sheet from oven. Place pan on cooling rack. Let stand for 2 to 3 minutes. Cut each pizza into 4 pieces using a pizza cutter, if you like.

Serve with...
torn salad greens tossed with croutons and your favorite salad dressing, and milk.

SOUPER WHEELIES

Prep: 30 minutes
Cook: 22 minutes
Makes 4 servings.

Who said you can't do wheelies at the dinner table?

Ingredients

- 1 small onion
- 12 ounces lean ground beef or ground turkey
- 1 14½-ounce can beef broth
- 1 14½-ounce can Italian-style stewed tomatoes
- 1½ cups water
- ¾ cup wagon wheel macaroni (ruote pasta)
- 1 cup frozen whole kernel corn*
- 1 cup frozen cut green beans*
- 1 teaspoon dried basil, crushed
- ½ teaspoon dried oregano, crushed

Utensils

Cutting board
Sharp knife
Large saucepan
Wooden spoon
Colander
Hot pads
Medium bowl
Can opener
Measuring cups
Measuring spoons
Fork

Nutrition Facts Per Serving

Calories	289
Total fat	9 g
Saturated fat	3 g
Cholesterol	54 mg
Sodium	736 mg
Carbohydrate	32 g
Fiber	0 g
Protein	21 g

"I'd like to eat this soup outside in the cold," says Theresa, one of the kid-testers. "It warms me up!"

1. On the cutting board use the sharp knife to cut onion into small pieces.

2. Put ground meat in the saucepan; use the wooden spoon to break up meat. Add onion pieces. Put the saucepan on a burner. Turn the burner to medium-high heat. Cook until no pink color is left in meat, stirring now and then with the wooden spoon. Turn off burner. Remove saucepan from burner.

3. Place colander over bowl. Spoon meat into the colander and let fat drain into the bowl. Spoon meat back into saucepan. Put fat in a container to throw away.

4. Open cans of beef broth and tomatoes. Do not drain tomatoes; save for Step 6.

5. Stir beef broth and water into meat. Put the saucepan on a burner. Turn the burner to high heat. Heat until mixture begins to boil. Add macaroni and turn burner to medium-high heat. Cook, uncovered, for 12 minutes. Stir macaroni mixture often with the wooden spoon.

6. Turn the burner to medium heat. Stir in corn, green beans, basil, oregano, and undrained tomatoes. Return to boiling, then turn the burner to medium-low heat. Cover and cook about 10 minutes or until vegetables are tender when poked with a fork. Stir mixture now and then with the wooden spoon. Turn off burner. Remove saucepan from burner.

^If you like, use one 10-ounce package or 2 cups of frozen mixed vegetables in place of frozen corn and green beans.

Serve with... crisp breadsticks, chocolate chip cookies for dessert, and milk.

L U N C H

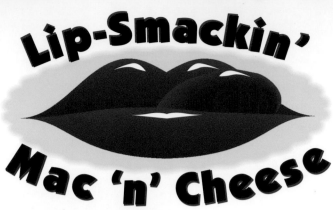

Lip-Smackin' Mac 'n' Cheese

Prep: 15 minutes
Cook: 12 minutes
Makes 3 servings.

Use your noodle and add 1 cup of frozen veggies with the macaroni to make a meal-in-one.

Ingredients

- 1 onion
- 6 ounces American cheese slices
- 2 cups corkscrew macaroni (rotini) or elbow macaroni
- ½ cup skim milk
- Dash pepper

Utensils

Cutting board
Sharp knife
Measuring cups
Large saucepan
Colander
Hot pads
Wooden spoon

Nutrition Facts Per Serving	
Calories	412
Total fat	19 g
Saturated fat	11 g
Cholesterol	55 mg
Sodium	833 mg
Carbohydrate	40 g
Fiber	1 g
Protein	20 g

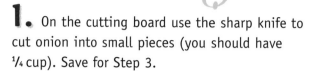

1. On the cutting board use the sharp knife to cut onion into small pieces (you should have ¼ cup). Save for Step 3.

2. Tear cheese slices into bite-size pieces. Save for Step 5.

3. Cook macaroni in the saucepan following the package directions, except add onion to water along with the uncooked macaroni so they cook together. (To test macaroni for doneness, remove one piece, let it cool slightly, and bite into it. The center will be soft, not chewy.) When macaroni is cooked, turn off the burner. Remove saucepan from burner.

4. Place colander in sink. Carefully pour macaroni mixture into the colander to drain water.

5. Return warm macaroni mixture to saucepan. Use wooden spoon to stir in cheese, milk, and pepper.

6. Put saucepan on a burner. Turn the burner to medium heat. Cook for 4 to 5 minutes or until cheese is melted, stirring all the time. Turn off burner. Remove saucepan from burner.

L
U
N
C
H

Smack·O·Meter

YUMMY AWESOME LIP-SMACKIN'

Serve with...
cooked green beans, rolls with jam, fresh pears, and milk.

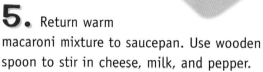

Start to finish:
5 to 10 minutes each
Makes 1 serving each.

BREAD-WINNING SPREADS

Your daily bread never tasted this good.

Fruit and Cheese Spread

Put ½ of an 8-ounce tub *cream cheese,* ¼ cup *mixed dried fruit bits,* and 2 tablespoons *shelled sunflower seeds* in a small mixing bowl. Stir with a wooden spoon until mixed. Split and toast English muffins. Spread cheese mixture on muffin halves.

Ham and Cheese Roll-Ups

Spread a little *mustard* on a 7- or 8-inch *flour tortilla,* if you like. Add 1 slice of thinly sliced *cooked ham,* 1 slice of *Swiss cheese,* and ¼ cup finely chopped *broccoli.* Tightly roll up tortilla. Microwave on 100% power (high) for 1 minute or until warm.

Caitlyn and Kale voted for the open-face sandwiches because "they show what's inside."

Berry Bagels

Toast a *presplit bagel;* let it cool a little. Spread bagel halves with *cream cheese with strawberries.* Top halves with a layer of sliced fresh *strawberries.*

10

Apples and Peanut Butter

Toast 2 slices of *raisin bread.* Spread 1 slice of bread with *peanut butter.* Top with a layer of thinly sliced *apples* and second slice of raisin bread.

10

g E S

TANGLED TWISTERS

Sugar and spice make these chewy pretzels especially nice.

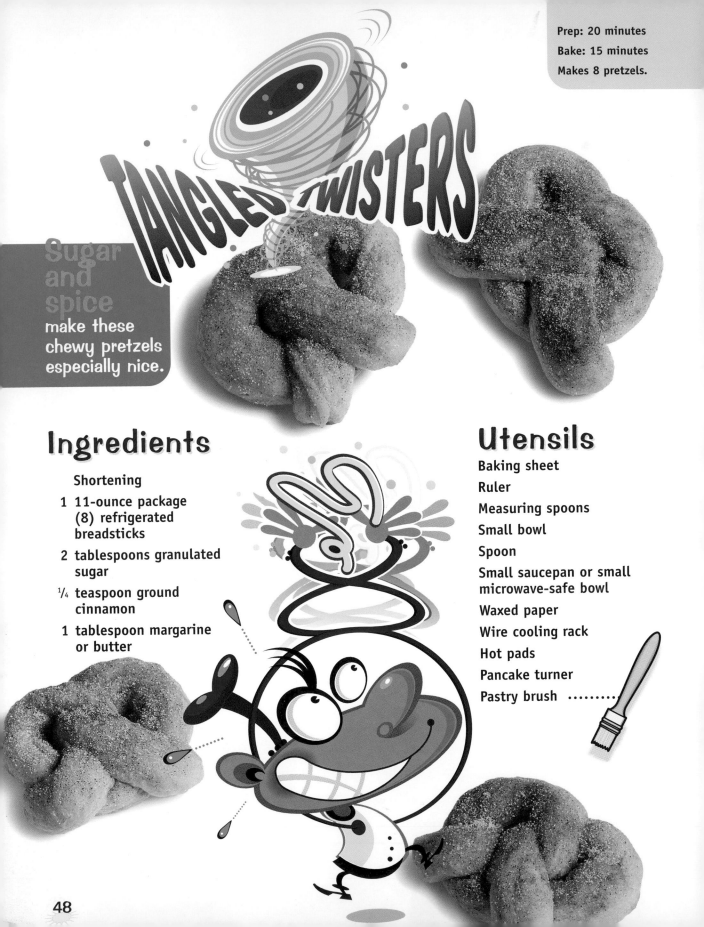

Ingredients

Shortening

1 11-ounce package (8) refrigerated breadsticks

2 tablespoons granulated sugar

¼ teaspoon ground cinnamon

1 tablespoon margarine or butter

Utensils

Baking sheet

Ruler

Measuring spoons

Small bowl

Spoon

Small saucepan or small microwave-safe bowl

Waxed paper

Wire cooling rack

Hot pads

Pancake turner

Pastry brush ·········

Nutrition Facts Per Pretzel	
Calories	130
Total fat	4 g
Saturated fat	1 g
Cholesterol	0 mg
Sodium	254 mg
Carbohydrate	20 g
Fiber	1 g
Protein	3 g

"They're terrific," according to kid-testers Abby and Ryan, who decided the pretzels taste like cinnamon rolls and are good for snacks or for breakfast.

1. Turn on oven to 350°. Grease the baking sheet with shortening. Save until Step 3.

2. Open the breadstick package and remove breadsticks. Gently pull or roll each breadstick on the countertop to make a rope of dough about 20 inches long. Shape each rope of dough into a pretzel by crossing one end over the other, forming a circle and leaving 4 inch tails(a). Holding a tail in each hand, twist once at the crossover point(b). Carefully lift the tails and place over the center of the circle(c). Place the ends of the tails over the circle edge and tuck them under to make a pretzel shape(d). Press ends to seal.

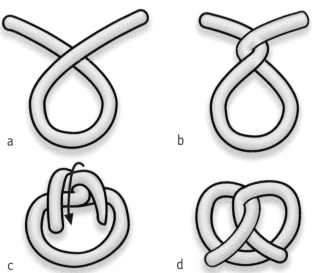

a

b

c

d

3. Place pretzels on prepared baking sheet about 2 inches apart. Put baking sheet in oven. Bake for 15 to 18 minutes or until pretzels are light brown.

4. While pretzels are baking, put sugar and cinnamon in the bowl. Stir with the spoon to mix. Save until Step 6.

5. Put the margarine or butter in the saucepan. Put saucepan on a burner. Turn burner to low heat. Cook until margarine or butter is melted. Turn off burner. Remove saucepan from burner. Or, put margarine or butter in the microwave-safe bowl. Cover bowl with waxed paper. Microwave on 100% power (high) for 20 seconds or until margarine is melted. Using hot pads, remove bowl from microwave.

6. Place cooling rack over waxed paper. When pretzels are baked, turn off oven. Remove baking sheet from oven with hot pads. Use the pancake turner to transfer pretzels from baking sheet to cooling rack. Use the pastry brush to spread melted margarine or butter over tops of pretzels. Sprinkle with sugar-cinnamon mixture. Serve warm.

OOEY GOOEY CHEWIES

Start to finish: 20 minutes

Makes 24 bars.

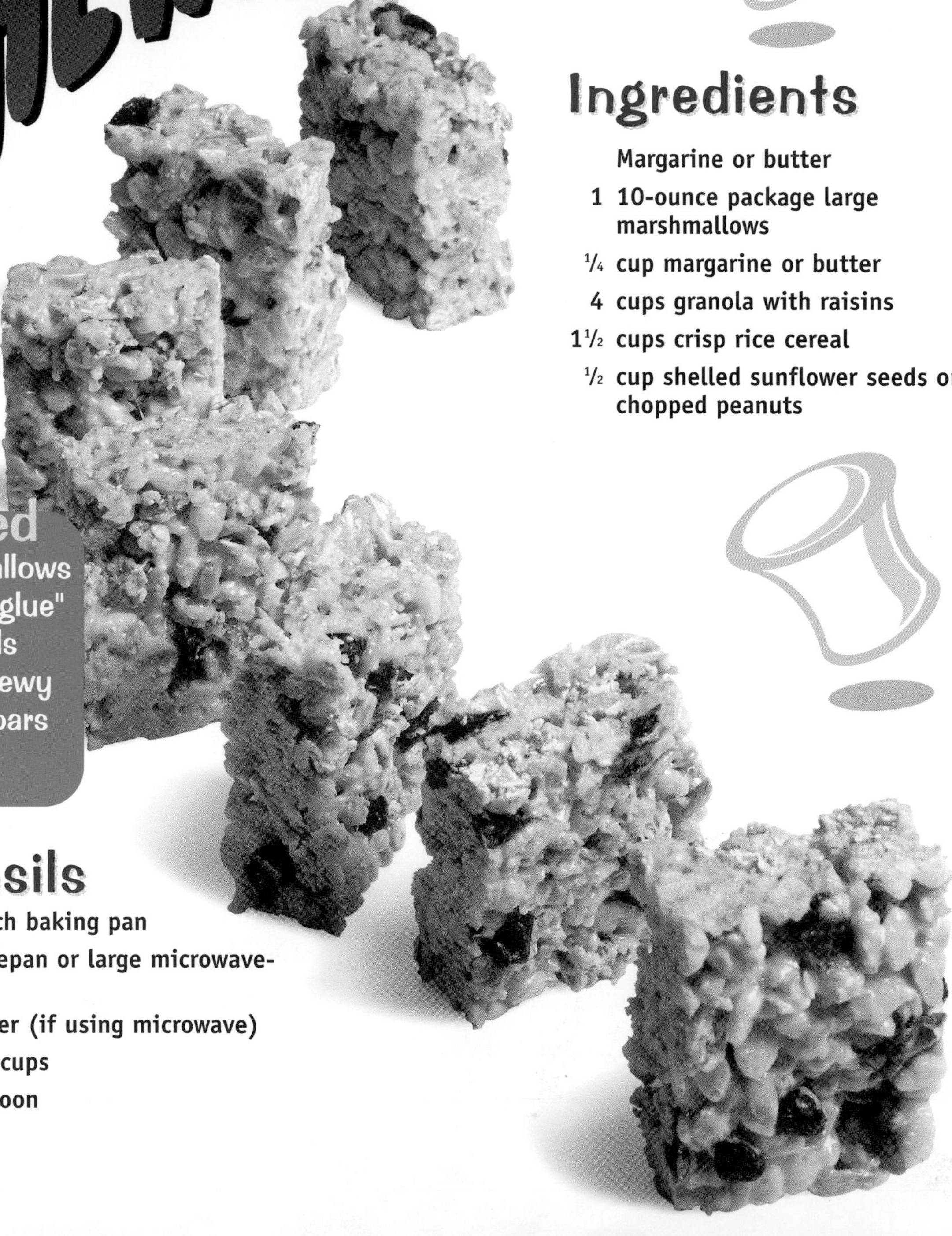

Ingredients

- Margarine or butter
- 1 10-ounce package large marshmallows
- 1/4 cup margarine or butter
- 4 cups granola with raisins
- 1 1/2 cups crisp rice cereal
- 1/2 cup shelled sunflower seeds or chopped peanuts

Melted marshmallows are the "glue" that holds these chewy granola bars together.

Utensils

- 13x9x2-inch baking pan
- Large saucepan or large microwave-safe bowl
- Waxed paper (if using microwave)
- Measuring cups
- Wooden spoon
- Knife
- Hot pads

Nutrition Facts Per Bar

Calories	162
Total fat	7 g
Saturated fat	3 g
Cholesterol	0 mg
Sodium	84 mg
Carbohydrate	24 g
Fiber	1 g
Protein	3 g

1. Grease the pan with some margarine or butter. Save until Step 4.

2. Put marshmallows and the ¼ cup margarine or butter in the saucepan. Put saucepan on a burner. Turn burner to medium-low heat. Cook until marshmallows are melted, stirring all the time with the wooden spoon. Turn off burner. Remove saucepan from burner.

3. Stir in granola with raisins, crisp rice cereal, and sunflower seeds or peanuts.

4. Transfer mixture to the prepared baking pan. Press with buttered hands to make it even. Let mixture cool. Cut into bars with the knife.

Microwave directions

Put marshmallows and margarine in a large microwave-safe bowl. Microwave, uncovered, on 100% power (high) for 1½ to 2 minutes or until marshmallows are smooth, stopping the microwave and stirring after 30 seconds and again after 1 minute. Using hot pads, remove bowl from microwave. Stir in granola with raisins, rice cereal, and sunflower seeds or peanuts with a wooden spoon. Continue as directed in Step 4.

CRAZY Quesadillas

Prep: 15 minutes
Cook: 5 minutes each
Makes 4 servings.

Nutrition Facts Per Serving	
Calories	138
Total fat	7 g
Saturated fat	4 g
Cholesterol	17 mg
Sodium	239 mg
Carbohydrate	11 g
Fiber	1 g
Protein	7 g

It's **fiesta time,** not siesta time, with these easy, tasty tortillas filled with cheese and refried beans.

Ingredients

- ¼ **cup refried beans**
- 4 **6- to 8-inch flour tortillas**
- ⅔ **cup shredded colby-and-Monterey-Jack cheese**
- **Salsa, if you like**

Utensils

Can opener
Measuring cups
Table knife
Medium skillet
Pancake turner
Kitchen scissors

1. Use the table knife to spread half of the refried beans on 1 tortilla.

2. Place bean-topped tortilla in the skillet with the bean side up. Put skillet on a burner. Turn the burner to medium heat. Sprinkle half of the cheese over tortilla. Top with 1 plain tortilla.

3. Cook over medium heat about 3 minutes or until cheese begins to melt. Use the pancake turner to turn quesadilla over. Cook 2 minutes more. Use pancake turner to remove quesadilla from skillet. Repeat with remaining tortillas, refried beans, and cheese. Turn off burner. Remove skillet from burner. Use pancake turner to remove quesadilla from skillet.

4. Use the scissors to cut each quesadilla into 6 triangles. Serve with salsa, if you like.

Prep: 15 minutes

Freeze: 4 hours

Makes 10 pops.

Nutrition Facts Per Pop

Calories	85
Total fat	1 g
Saturated fat	1 g
Cholesterol	4 mg
Sodium	204 mg
Carbohydrate	17 g
Fiber	0 g
Protein	2 g

Candy sprinkles make these the top of pops.

1. Put the paper cups in the baking pan. Sprinkle some decorative candies in the bottom of each paper cup.

2. Put the pudding mix in the mixing bowl. Add milk. Use the wire whisk or rotary beater to beat pudding until well mixed. Spoon pudding into paper cups.

3. Cover each cup with foil. Use the knife to make a small hole in center of foil. Slide a wooden stick through the hole and into the pudding in the cup.

4. Put the baking pan in the freezer. Freeze 4 to 6 hours or until pudding pops are firm. Remove from freezer. Remove foil and tear paper cups away from the pudding pops.

Ingredients

Small multicolored decorative candies

1 4-serving-size package instant chocolate pudding mix

2½ cups chocolate-flavored milk

Utensils

10 3-ounce paper cups

8x8- or 9x9-inch baking pan

Medium mixing bowl

Measuring cup

Wire whisk or rotary beater

Large spoon

Foil

Small sharp knife

10 wooden sticks

COSMIC CARAMEL CORN

Prep: 15 minutes
Bake: 15 minutes
Makes about 4 cups.

Nutrition Facts Per ½ Cup	
Calories	191
Total fat	12 g
Saturated fat	2 g
Cholesterol	0 mg
Sodium	60 mg
Carbohydrate	19 g
Fiber	2 g
Protein	3 g

Ingredients

- **6 cups popped popcorn (about 3 tablespoons unpopped)**
- **3 tablespoons margarine or butter**
- **¼ cup light-colored corn syrup**
- **1 tablespoon molasses**
- **1 cup dry roasted cashews, peanuts, or shelled sunflower seeds**

Utensils

Measuring cups and spoons
13x9x2-inch baking pan
Small saucepan or small microwave-safe bowl
Waxed paper (if using microwave)
Wooden spoon
Hot pads
Serving bowl

1. Turn on oven to 325°. Place the popped popcorn in the baking pan. Save until Step 4.

2. Put margarine or butter in the saucepan. Put saucepan on a burner. Turn burner to low heat. Heat until margarine or butter melts. Turn off burner. Remove saucepan from burner. Or, put margarine or butter in the microwave-safe bowl. Cover bowl with waxed paper. Microwave on 100% power (high) for 20 to 30 seconds or until margarine is melted. Using hot pads, remove bowl from microwave.

3. Using a wooden spoon, stir corn syrup and molasses into melted margarine or butter.

4. Slowly pour the corn syrup mixture over popcorn in baking pan. Use the wooden spoon to toss the popcorn and coat it as evenly as possible with the corn syrup mixture.

5. Put baking pan in oven. Bake for 15 minutes, stirring with a wooden spoon about every 5 minutes; use hot pads when removing the pan from the oven each time. Turn off oven. Remove pan from oven with hot pads.

6. Pour caramel corn into the serving bowl. Stir in nuts or sunflower seeds with the wooden spoon. Let caramel corn cool. Store in a tightly covered container at room temperature.

Start to finish:
10 minutes
Makes about 4 cups.

Nutrition Facts Per Cup
(with Parmesan seasoning)

Calories	91
Total fat	7 g
Saturated fat	2 g
Cholesterol	2 mg
Sodium	126 mg
Carbohydrate	5 g
Fiber	0 g
Protein	2 g

DIVE-IN POPCORN

Ingredients

2 **tablespoons margarine or butter**

4 **cups popped popcorn**

Parmesan, Taco, or Cheese Seasoning

Utensils

Small saucepan or small microwave-safe bowl

Waxed paper (if using microwave)

Large plastic bag

Measuring spoons

1. Put the margarine or butter in the small saucepan. Put the saucepan on a burner. Turn burner to low heat. Heat until margarine melts. Turn off burner. Remove saucepan from burner. Or, put margarine in the bowl; cover bowl with waxed paper. Microwave on 100% power (high) 20 to 30 seconds or until margarine is melted.

2. Put popped popcorn in the plastic bag. Pour melted margarine over the popcorn. Sprinkle one of the seasonings over popcorn in bag. Close the bag tightly. Shake well to mix.

Taco Seasoning
Sprinkle 1 teaspoon *taco seasoning mix* over buttered popcorn in plastic bag.

Take a dive off the high board and **grab a big handful** of one of these corny snacks.

Parmesan Seasoning
Sprinkle 2 tablespoons grated *Parmesan cheese* and 1 tablespoon finely snipped *parsley,* if you like, over buttered popcorn in plastic bag.

Cheese Seasoning
Sprinkle 1 tablespoon *grated American cheese food* over buttered popcorn in plastic bag.

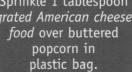

S
N
A
C
K
S

55

Hit the Trail MIX

**Nutrition Facts Per
½ Cup Serving**

Calories	234
Total fat	12 g
Saturated fat	2 g
Cholesterol	0 mg
Sodium	135 mg
Carbohydrate	29 g
Fiber	2 g
Protein	6 g

Hey, pardners— substitute ½ cup of your favorite cereal for the fruit snacks, and the trail boss may put this on your breakfast menu, too.

Ingredients

1½ cups puffed corn cereal, round toasted oat cereal, or crispy corn and rice cereal

1 cup honey-roasted peanuts

½ cup chewy fruit snacks or candy-coated milk chocolate pieces

½ cup raisins

Utensils

Measuring cups

Plastic bag

1. Put the cereal, peanuts, fruit snacks or chocolate pieces, and raisins in the plastic bag. Close the bag tightly. Shake well to mix.

2. Store mix in the plastic bag in a cool, dry place for up to 2 weeks.

Start to finish:
5 minutes

Makes about 2 cups.

Nutrition Facts Per Tablespoon Dip

Calories	11
Total fat	0 g
Saturated fat	0 g
Cholesterol	0 mg
Sodium	80 mg
Carbohydrate	2 g
Fiber	0 g
Protein	1 g

I Can't Believe I Like My Veggies DIP

Ingredients

1 8-ounce carton fat-free dairy sour cream or one 8-ounce tub cream cheese

1 8-ounce carton plain fat-free yogurt

1 0.4-ounce envelope Ranch dry salad dressing mix (does not contain butter-milk solids)

Cut-up vegetables

Utensils

Medium mixing bowl

Wooden spoon

Electric mixer, if you like

Take the plunge with carrots, celery, green pepper strips, broccoli flowerets, cherry tomatoes, or cucumber rounds. They're all yummy with dip.

1. Put the sour cream or cream cheese, yogurt, and dressing mix in the bowl. Stir together with the wooden spoon. If using cream cheese, beat with an electric mixer on medium speed until smooth. Serve dip with cut-up vegetables.

SNACKS

57

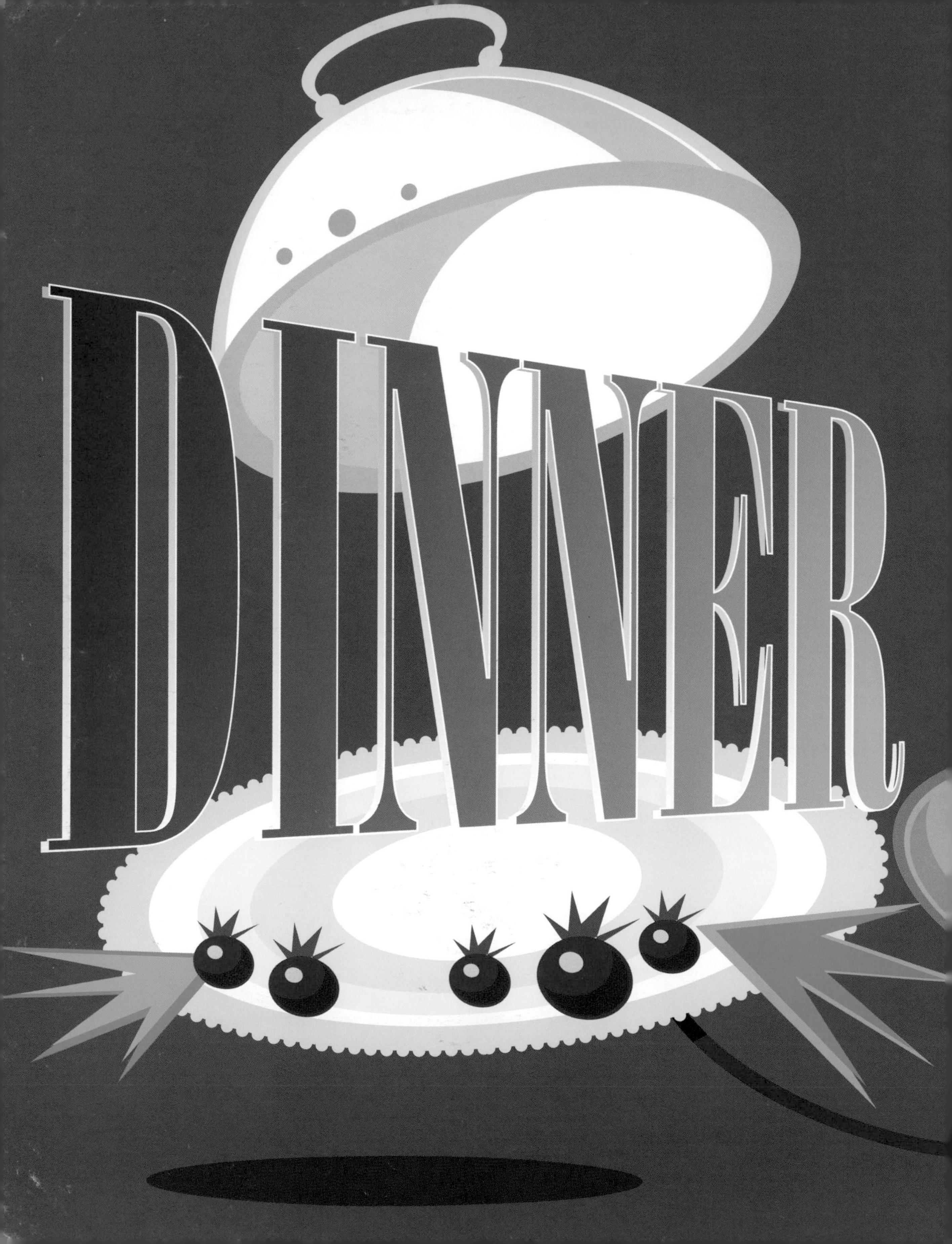
DINNER

is served

BELLY-BUSTER BURGER

Utensils

Waxed paper
Ruler
Large skillet
Pancake turner
Hot pads

Forget fast food and make your own quarter-pound burgers. And if you please, top them with cheese.

Ingredients

1 pound lean ground beef
Salt
Pepper
4 split hamburger buns

Topping choices: catsup, mustard, barbecue sauce, mayonnaise or salad dressing, lettuce leaves, tomato slices, salsa, and/or dill pickle slices or sweet pickle slices

Nutrition Facts Per Burger

Calories	306
Total fat	13 g
Saturated fat	5 g
Cholesterol	71 mg
Sodium	318 mg
Carbohydrate	22 g
Fiber	0 g
Protein	24 g

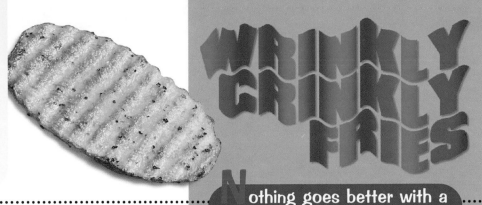

WRINKLY CRINKLY FRIES

Nothing goes better with a burger than fries.

1. Place a piece of waxed paper on the counter or table. Put ground beef on waxed paper. Use your hands to divide meat into 4 equal portions. Shape each portion into a flat, round patty that measures about 3½ inches across. Put hamburger patties in the skillet.

2. Put the skillet on a burner. Turn the burner to medium heat. Cook about 7 minutes or until hamburgers are brown on the bottom. To check, lift hamburgers with the pancake turner and peek underneath.

3. Use the pancake turner to turn over each hamburger. Sprinkle hamburgers with salt and pepper. Cook for 4 to 7 minutes more or until no pink color is left in hamburgers. Turn off burner. Remove skillet from burner.

4. Toast hamburger buns in the oven, if you like (see note, page 77). Place bottom halves of the hamburger buns on a serving plate. Use the pancake turner to lift hamburgers from skillet and set them on the bottom buns. Add toppings of your choice. Cover with bun tops.

Serve with... coleslaw, brownies for dessert, and milk.

1. Scrub 3 *baking potatoes* with a vegetable brush, leaving peel on. Cut potatoes into ¼-inch-thick slices with a crinkle cutter or sharp knife. Put potato slices in a large plastic bag.

2. Put 2 tablespoons *cooking oil* and ½ teaspoon *herb-pepper seasoning* or *lemon-pepper seasoning*, or ¼ teaspoon *salt* in a small bowl. Mix well. Add oil mixture to potatoes in bag. Seal or tie plastic bag closed. Shake well to mix potatoes with seasoning mixture.

3. Put potatoes in a single layer in a baking pan. Bake in a 450° oven about 25 minutes or until potatoes are lightly browned and tender.

61

In **Italian**, pizza means "pie." In English, it means the yummiest way to eat your veggies.

Ingredients

Shortening
1½ cups all-purpose flour
½ cup whole wheat flour
¼ cup yellow cornmeal
1 teaspoon baking powder
⅔ cup milk
¼ cup cooking oil
1 medium green sweet pepper
1 small onion
1½ cups fresh mushrooms
1 8-ounce can pizza sauce
⅓ cup sliced pitted ripe olives, if you like
1½ cups shredded mozzarella cheese (6 ounces)

Utensils

12-inch pizza pan
Measuring cups
Measuring spoons
Medium mixing bowl
Wooden spoon
Wooden board or pastry cloth
Rolling pin
Hot pads
Wire cooling rack
Cutting board
Sharp knife
Can opener
Spoon

Nutrition Facts Per Serving

Calories	533
Total fat	23 g
Saturated fat	7 g
Cholesterol	27 mg
Sodium	641 mg
Carbohydrate	62 g
Fiber	4 g
Protein	21 g

Serve with...

tossed salad greens with ranch dressing, peanut butter cookies for dessert, and milk.

1. Turn on oven to 425°. Grease the pizza pan with shortening. Save until Step 4.

2. For pizza dough,* put all-purpose flour, whole wheat flour, cornmeal, and baking powder in the mixing bowl. Stir with a wooden spoon until mixed. Add milk and oil. Stir until well mixed.

3. Sprinkle a generous amount of flour on a wooden board or pastry cloth. Put pizza dough on the floured surface. Knead 10 to 12 times. (To knead, pat dough into a circle on the floured surface. Fold dough in half and push it down and away from you with the heels of your hands. Turn dough, fold it over, and push down again. Repeat this 8 to 10 times.)

4. Roll out dough with the rolling pin to a 12-inch circle. Press kneaded dough into pizza pan, building up edges into a rim. Put pizza pan in oven. Bake for 12 to 15 minutes or until pizza crust is light brown. Use hot pads to remove pizza pan from oven. Place on the cooling rack.

5. On the cutting board use the sharp knife to cut the green pepper in half from top to bottom. Pull off the stem and throw away. Remove seeds and soft white parts from inside the pepper halves. Cut pepper halves into small pieces (you should have about ¾ cup). On the cutting board use the sharp knife to cut the onion into small pieces (you should have about ⅓ cup). On the cutting board use the sharp knife to slice the mushrooms.

6. Use the can opener to open can of pizza sauce. Carefully spoon pizza sauce over crust. Top sauce with green pepper, onion, mushrooms, and olives, if you like. Sprinkle with cheese.

7. Use hot pads to put pizza pan back in oven. Bake for 10 to 15 minutes more or until cheese is melted and bubbly. Turn off oven. Use hot pads to remove pizza pan from oven. Let stand on cooling rack for 5 minutes.

Note: If you like, use refrigerated pizza dough or prepared bread shells in place of the homemade crust.

LICKETY-SPLIT LASAGNA

Prep: 30 minutes
Bake: 1 hour
Makes 6 servings.

Two, four, six, eight—dig in, don't wait!

Ingredients

12 ounces ground beef

2½ cups spaghetti sauce

6 lasagna noodles

1½ cups cottage cheese

1½ cups shredded mozzarella cheese (6 ounces)

2 tablespoons grated Parmesan cheese, if you like

Utensils

Medium skillet

Wooden spoon

Colander

Small mixing bowl

Measuring cups

2-quart rectangular baking dish

Foil

Hot pads

Wire cooling rack

Tongs

64

Nutrition Facts Per Serving	
Calories	430
Total fat	20 g
Saturated fat	8 g
Cholesterol	61 mg
Sodium	928 mg
Carbohydrate	33 g
Fiber	0 g
Protein	29 g

1. Turn on oven to 350°. Put ground beef in the skillet. Break up meat with a wooden spoon. Put skillet on a burner. Turn burner to medium-high heat. Cook until no pink color is left in meat, stirring now and then with the wooden spoon. Turn off burner. Remove skillet from burner.

2. Place colander over bowl. Spoon meat into colander and let fat drain into bowl. Spoon meat back into skillet. Put fat in a container to throw away.

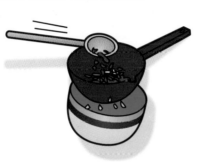

3. Spoon 1 cup of the spaghetti sauce in the bottom of the baking dish. Stir remaining spaghetti sauce into meat in skillet. Put skillet on a burner. Turn burner to medium heat. Cook until hot, stirring now and then with the wooden spoon. Turn off burner. Remove meat mixture from burner.

4. Place 2 uncooked noodles on sauce in bottom of dish. Spread one-third of the meat mixture on top of noodles. Spread ¾ cup of the cottage cheese over meat. Sprinkle ½ cup of the mozzarella cheese over cottage cheese.

Add another layer of 2 uncooked noodles, one-third of the meat mixture, the rest of the cottage cheese, and ½ cup of the mozzarella cheese. Layer remaining uncooked noodles, meat mixture, and mozzarella cheese. Finally, sprinkle Parmesan cheese over top, if you like.

5. Cover baking dish with foil. Put covered dish in oven. Bake for 1 hour. Turn off oven. Use hot pads to remove baking dish from oven. Let stand on a cooling rack with foil cover in place for 15 minutes. Using tongs, carefully remove foil from dish so steam escapes away from you.

Serve with... Italian green beans, breadsticks, lettuce wedge salads with Italian salad dressing, sherbet for dessert, and milk.

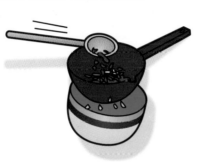

PLUCKER POWER STIR-FRY

It's the sweet-and-sour sauce that gives this chicken dinner its pucker power.

Ingredients

- 1 medium red or green sweet pepper
- 1 small carrot
- 1 8-ounce can pineapple chunks (juice-packed)
- ½ cup bottled sweet-and-sour sauce
- 12 ounces skinless, boneless chicken breast halves
- 1½ cups quick-cooking rice
- 1 tablespoon cooking oil

Utensils

Cutting board

Sharp knife

Vegetable peeler ·····

Can opener

Strainer

2 small mixing bowls

Measuring cups

Measuring spoons

Wooden spoon

Medium saucepan with lid

Large skillet

Pancake turner

Hot pads

Nutrition Facts Per Serving

Calories	350
Total fat	6 g
Saturated fat	1 g
Cholesterol	45 mg
Sodium	154 mg
Carbohydrate	54 g
Fiber	1 g
Protein	20 g

Serve with...
cooked broccoli spears, fortune cookies for dessert, and milk.

1. On the cutting board use the sharp knife to cut the red or green pepper in half from top to bottom. Pull off the stem and throw away. Remove seeds and soft white parts from inside the pepper halves and throw away. Cut pepper halves into bite-size pieces. Save until Step 7.

2. Peel carrot with vegetable peeler. On the cutting board use the sharp knife to cut the carrot into thin slices. Save until Step 7.

3. Use can opener to open pineapple. Place strainer over a mixing bowl. Empty can of pineapple into strainer and drain juice, saving the juice in the bowl. In another mixing bowl put 2 tablespoons of the saved pineapple juice and the sweet-and-sour sauce. Use the wooden spoon to stir the mixture together. Save until Step 8. Discard remaining pineapple juice.

4. On the cutting board use the sharp knife to cut chicken into bite-size pieces. Save until Step 7.

5. Put 1½ cups *water* in the saucepan. Put saucepan on a burner. Turn burner to medium-high heat and bring water to boiling. Turn off burner. Remove saucepan from burner. Carefully add the rice to boiling water, stirring with a wooden spoon. Cover saucepan with lid and let rice stand while cooking chicken and vegetables.

6. Pour oil into the skillet. Put skillet on a burner. Turn burner to medium-high heat. Heat for 1 minute or until oil is hot.

7. Carefully add pepper pieces and carrot slices to oil in skillet. Cook for 1 minute, lifting and turning all the time with the pancake turner. Add chicken pieces. Cook 3 to 4 minutes or until chicken is tender and no pink remains in the center, lifting and turning all the time with the pancake turner.

8. Add sweet-and-sour sauce mixture and drained pineapple chunks. Cook 1 minute or until hot, stirring now and then with a wooden spoon. Turn off burner. Remove skillet from burner. Serve chicken mixture over hot rice.

Crunchy Munchy Chicken

Prep: 25 minutes
Bake: 45 minutes
Makes 4 servings.

Thanks to the cornmeal coating, the chicken stays crunchy on the outside.

Ingredients

2 pounds meaty chicken pieces (breasts, thighs, and drumsticks)

2 cups corn bread stuffing mix

1 egg

2 tablespoons milk

2 tablespoons honey, if you like

2 tablespoons margarine or butter

Utensils

Paper towels

Measuring cups

Measuring spoons

Plastic bag

Rolling pin

9-inch pie plate

Mixing bowl

Fork

13x9x2-inch baking pan

Small saucepan

Hot pads

Knife

Nutrition Facts Per Serving	
Calories	430
Total fat	16 g
Saturated fat	4 g
Cholesterol	146 mg
Sodium	649 mg
Carbohydrate	34 g
Fiber	0 g
Protein	36 g

1. Turn on oven to 375°. Remove skin from chicken by pulling it away from meat. Throw skin away. Rinse chicken under cold water. Pat dry with paper towels. Save until Step 4.

2. Put stuffing mix in the plastic bag. Seal or tie plastic bag closed. Use the rolling pin to crush stuffing mix. Pour stuffing mix into the pie plate.

3. Crack the egg into mixing bowl. Beat egg with the fork until white and yolk are mixed. Add milk to beaten egg. Stir in honey with the fork, if you like.

4. Dip each piece of chicken into egg mixture, turning to coat completely.

5. Roll each chicken piece in crumb mixture. Press crumbs onto chicken pieces so that they stick. Place chicken pieces, meaty sides up, in the baking pan. Sprinkle chicken with any remaining stuffing mix.

6. Put margarine or butter in the saucepan. Put pan on a burner. Turn burner to low heat. Cook until margarine is melted. Turn off burner. Remove saucepan from heat. Drizzle melted margarine over the chicken pieces.

7. Put baking pan in oven. Bake for 45 to 55 minutes or until no pink color is left in the center of a chicken piece. (To check chicken for doneness, use hot pads to remove pan from oven and cut into a chicken piece with a knife to check that chicken isn't pink.) Turn off oven. Let stand about 5 minutes before serving to cool slightly.

Serve with... hot cooked peas, cold crisp carrot sticks, dinner rolls with jam, and milk.

CHICKEN DIPPIN' STICKS

Prep: 25 minutes
Bake: 15 minutes
Makes 4 servings.

Dip these chicken sticks into some catsup, mustard, barbecue sauce, or salsa.

Ingredients

Shortening

4 medium skinless, boneless chicken breast halves (about 1 pound total)

1 cup bite-size cheese crackers (regular or reduced-fat)

$\frac{1}{4}$ cup fine dry bread crumbs

$\frac{1}{2}$ cup buttermilk or milk

Utensils

13x9x2-inch baking pan

Cutting board

Sharp knife

Measuring cups

Large plastic bag

Rolling pin

9-inch pie plate

Wooden spoon

Medium mixing bowl

Hot pads

Nutrition Facts Per Serving	
Calories	158
Total fat	4 g
Saturated fat	1 g
Cholesterol	61 mg
Sodium	132 mg
Carbohydrate	6 g
Fiber	0 g
Protein	23 g

Kid-tester Beth says these are "better than a burger."

1. Turn on the oven to 400°. Grease the baking pan with a little shortening. Save until Step 5.

2. On the cutting board use the sharp knife to cut each chicken breast half into 6 strips. Save until Step 4.

3. Put crackers in the plastic bag. Seal or tie plastic bag closed. Use the rolling pin to crush the crackers. Pour the crushed crackers into the pie plate. Add bread crumbs. Stir with a wooden spoon until mixed. (Or, leave cracker crumbs in bag. Add bread crumbs to cracker crumbs and shake to combine.) Save until Step 5.

4. Pour buttermilk or milk into the mixing bowl. Dip each piece of chicken into the milk, turning to coat completely.

5. Roll each chicken piece in crumb mixture in pie plate. (Or, if crumb mixture is in the plastic bag, drop a few strips at a time into crumbs and shake to coat.) Press crumbs onto chicken pieces so that they stick. Place coated chicken pieces in greased baking pan.

6. Put baking pan in the oven. Bake for 15 to 20 minutes or until no pink color is left in the center of the chicken and the crumb mixture is golden brown. (To check for doneness, use hot pads to remove pan from oven and cut into a chicken piece with a clean knife.) Turn off oven.

Serve with... mashed potatoes, cooked carrot slices, crisp pickles, and milk.

CHAMPION CHILI

It's the cook's choice—
you can make this gold star chili with or without meat.*

Ingredients

1 15-ounce can pinto, kidney, or garbanzo beans

1 14½-ounce can stewed tomatoes or whole tomatoes, undrained

1 15-ounce can chili beans, undrained

1 medium green sweet pepper

1 medium onion

1 cup tomato juice

2 to 3 teaspoons chili powder

¼ cup shredded cheddar cheese, if you like

Utensils

Can opener
Colander
Kitchen scissors
Cutting board
Sharp knife
Large saucepan with lid
Wooden spoon
Hot pads

Nutrition Facts Per Serving	
Calories	216
Total fat	3 g
Saturated fat	0 g
Cholesterol	0 mg
Sodium	1,311 mg
Fiber	10 g
Protein	11 g

Our kid-testers, Lori, Eva, Erin, and Tyler, were unanimous— chili makes a tip-top dip for tortilla chips.

1. Use the can opener to open can of pinto, kidney, or garbanzo beans. Place colander in sink. Empty beans into colander. Rinse under cold water and drain water. Save until Step 6.

2. Use can opener to open cans of tomatoes and chili beans. If using whole tomatoes, cut them up with scissors right in the can. Save until Step 4. Save chili beans until Step 6.

3. On the cutting board use the sharp knife to cut the green pepper in half from top to bottom. Pull off the stem and throw away. Remove seeds and soft white parts from inside pepper halves and throw away. Cut pepper halves into small pieces (you should have about ¾ cup). On the cutting board use the sharp knife to cut the onion into small pieces (you should have about ½ cup).

4. Put stewed tomatoes or undrained cut-up tomatoes, green pepper and onion pieces, tomato juice, and chili powder in the saucepan. Stir with the wooden spoon until mixed.

5. Put saucepan on a burner. Turn burner to medium-high heat. Bring tomato mixture to a boil. Turn burner to low heat. Cover pan with lid and simmer mixture for 10 minutes.

6. Add drained pinto, kidney, or garbanzo beans and undrained chili beans to saucepan. Stir mixture with wooden spoon. Cover and cook for 10 minutes more or until heated through. Turn off burner. Remove saucepan from burner. To serve, sprinkle some cheese on top of each serving, if you like.

Note: If you like a meaty chili, cook 8 ounces ground beef or turkey in a skillet. Drain fat in a colander and stir the meat into the chili along with the beans.

Serve with... crackers, pickle sticks, ice cream for dessert, and milk.

CRATER TATERS

Prep: 20 minutes

Bake: 1 hour (about 20 minutes if using the microwave)

Makes 4 servings.

A spud with a tempting topping explodes with flavor. Try one of these ideas or create your own concoction.

Utensils

Vegetable brush ··············
Fork
Hot pads

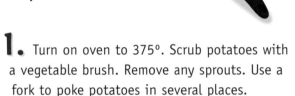

Ingredients

4 large baking potatoes (about 2 pounds total)

Choice of potato topping (see page 75)

1. Turn on oven to 375°. Scrub potatoes with a vegetable brush. Remove any sprouts. Use a fork to poke potatoes in several places.

2. Using hot pads, put potatoes on top rack in oven. Bake for 1 hour or until potatoes are tender when poked with the fork. Meanwhile, make your choice of potato topping.

3. When potatoes are tender, turn off oven. Use hot pads to remove potatoes from the oven. Use the fork to cut an X in the top of each potato, making an opening. Spoon selected topping onto the potatoes.

 ## Microwave directions

Cook poked potatoes on 100% power (high) 10 to 15 minutes or until almost tender, rearranging once. Let potatoes stand for 5 minutes before cutting them open and adding the toppings.

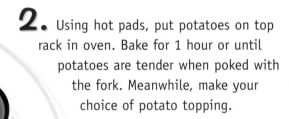

Nutrition Facts Per Serving with broccoli and cheese topping

Calories	275
Total fat	2 g
Saturated fat	1 g
Cholesterol	3 mg
Sodium	251 mg
Carbohydrate	58 g
Fiber	3 g
Protein	8 g

Utensils

Medium or small saucepan

Wooden spoon

Can opener

Measuring cups

Measuring spoons

Ham Alfredo

Put contents of one 10-ounce container *refrigerated Alfredo sauce for pasta* into a small saucepan. Stir in 1 cup diced *cooked ham*. Put saucepan on a burner. Turn burner to medium-low heat. Cook until mixture is hot, stirring now and then with a wooden spoon. Turn off burner. Remove saucepan from burner. Spoon mixture over baked potatoes. Sprinkle with snipped *parsley,* if you like.

Broccoli and Cheese

In a saucepan prepare one 10-ounce package *frozen cut broccoli in cheese sauce* as directed on the package. Turn off burner. Remove saucepan from burner. Spoon broccoli mixture over baked potatoes.

Serve with... crunchy carrot sticks, fruit salad, and milk.

Tex-Mex

Measure ½ cup *salsa* and ¼ cup *dairy sour cream* and/or *guacamole.* Spoon 2 tablespoons salsa on each baked potato. Spoon 1 tablespoon sour cream and/or guacamole on top of the salsa on each potato. Top with *shredded cheddar cheese,* if you like.

Chili and Cheese

Use can opener to open one 15-ounce can *chili with beans.* Put chili and ½ cup *shredded colby-and-Monterey-Jack cheese* or *cheddar cheese* in a medium saucepan. Put saucepan on a burner. Turn burner to medium-low heat. Cook until mixture is hot, stirring now and then with a wooden spoon. Turn off burner. Remove saucepan from burner. Spoon mixture over baked potatoes. Sprinkle with more shredded cheese and sliced *green onion,* if you like.

GobbleDygook
SANDWICHES

Prep: 15 minutes
Cook: 10 minutes
Makes 4 servings.

Smoked turkey
smothered in barbecue sauce and served on a bun may be sloppy, but who cares when it tastes this good?

Ingredients

10 ounces sliced cooked smoked turkey (about 2 cups)

1 medium carrot

½ cup bottled barbecue sauce

4 hamburger buns, split

Pickle slices, if you like

Utensils

Cutting board
Table knife
Vegetable peeler
Shredder
Measuring cup
Medium saucepan
Wooden spoon
Hot pads

Nutrition Facts Per Serving	
Calories	223
Total fat	4 g
Saturated fat	1 g
Cholesterol	30 mg
Sodium	1,212 mg
Carbohydrate	28 g
Fiber	1 g
Protein	19 g

Serve with...

corn, celery sticks, sliced banana layered with chocolate or vanilla pudding for dessert, and milk.

1. On a cutting board, use the table knife to cut turkey into strips.

2. Peel carrot with vegetable peeler; use the shredder to shred carrot. Put turkey, carrot, and barbecue sauce in saucepan. Stir together with the wooden spoon until mixed. Put saucepan on a burner. Turn burner to medium heat. Cook for 10 minutes or until mixture is hot, stirring now and then with a wooden spoon. Turn off burner. Remove saucepan from burner.

3. Toast the hamburger buns in the oven, if you like.* Place bottom halves of the hamburger buns on a serving plate. Spoon turkey mixture onto bottom buns. Top with pickle slices, if you like. Cover with bun tops.

Note: To toast hamburger buns, turn on the oven to broil. Place the split buns, cut sides up, on a baking sheet. Place baking sheet in the oven with the tops of the buns about 4 inches from the heat. Broil about 1 minute or until the buns are toasted, watching them carefully. Use hot pads to remove the pan from the oven. Turn off oven.

TOP-HEAVY VEGGIES

Prepare one 16-ounce package loose-pack frozen vegetables (your choice) following the package directions; drain thoroughly and add one of the sauces on these two pages.

Start to finish: about 20 minutes
Makes 4 servings.

It's a toss-up
which of the sauces you'll like the best on your veggies.

Herb Sauce

Toss hot vegetables with 2 tablespoons *Italian salad dressing*.

Salsa Cheese Sauce

Put ¼ cup bottled *process cheese sauce* and 2 tablespoons *salsa* in a small saucepan. Put saucepan on a burner. Turn burner to medium-low heat. Heat until cheese is melted, stirring all the time with a wooden spoon. Turn off burner. Remove saucepan from burner. Toss with hot vegetables.

Chunky Sweet-and-Sour Sauce

Put ⅓ cup bottled *sweet-and-sour sauce* and ¼ cup drained *crushed pineapple* in a small saucepan. Stir with a wooden spoon to mix. Put saucepan on a burner. Turn burner to medium-low heat. Heat until mixture is hot, stirring all the time with a wooden spoon. Turn off burner. Remove saucepan from burner. Toss with hot vegetables.

Oriental Sauce

Put 1 tablespoon *teriyaki sauce* or *soy sauce* and a dash of *ground ginger* in a small bowl. Stir with a spoon to mix. Pour over vegetables. Sprinkle with 1 teaspoon toasted *sesame seed.**

*Note: To toast sesame seeds, turn on oven to 350°. Spread seeds in a shallow baking pan. Put pan in oven. Bake for 5 to 10 minutes or until seeds are a light golden brown, watching carefully and stirring once or twice with a wooden spoon. Turn off oven. Use hot pads to remove baking pan from oven.

79

Hipper CHIPPERS

Prep: 20 minutes

Bake: 8 minutes per batch

Makes about 32 cookies.

Adding your favorite **chips or candy pieces** puts these cookies at the top of everyone's list.

Ingredients

- ½ cup butter or margarine
- ½ cup packed brown sugar
- ¼ cup granulated sugar
- ¼ teaspoon baking soda
- 1 egg
- 1 teaspoon vanilla
- 1¼ cups all-purpose flour
- 1 cup semisweet chocolate pieces and/or mini candy-coated semisweet chocolate pieces

Utensils

Table knife
Large mixing bowl
Measuring cups
Measuring spoons
Electric mixer
Rubber scraper
Wooden spoon
2 small spoons
Cookie sheet
Hot pads
Pancake turner
Wire cooling rack

Cool Daddy-o!

Nutrition Facts Per Cookie

Calories	85
Total fat	5 g
Saturated fat	2 g
Cholesterol	14 mg
Sodium	42 mg
Carbohydrate	11 g
Fiber	0 g
Protein	1 g

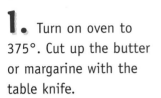

1. Turn on oven to 375°. Cut up the butter or margarine with the table knife.

2. Put butter or margarine in the mixing bowl. Beat with the electric mixer on medium speed about 30 seconds or until butter is softened. Stop the mixer. Add the brown sugar, granulated sugar, and baking soda. Beat on medium speed until combined, stopping the mixer occasionally and scraping the bowl with the rubber scraper. Stop the mixer.

3. Add the egg and the vanilla. Beat on medium speed until combined. Stop the mixer. Add half of the flour. Beat on medium speed until combined. Stop the mixer. Stir in the remaining flour and the chocolate pieces with the wooden spoon.

4. Scoop a rounded spoonful of dough with one of the spoons. Use the other spoon to push the dough onto the ungreased cookie sheet. Fill the cookie sheet with spoonfuls of dough, leaving about 2 inches between cookies.

5. Put the cookie sheet in the oven. Bake for 8 to 10 minutes or until cookie edges are light brown.

6. Use hot pads to remove cookie sheet from oven. Let cookies remain on cookie sheet for 1 minute. Use the pancake turner to transfer cookies to the cooling rack. Repeat with remaining dough, letting cookie sheet cool between batches or using a second cookie sheet. Turn off oven.

Triple Chippers: Prepare cookies as directed above, except use only ½ cup semisweet chocolate pieces. Add ½ cup *peanut butter pieces* and ¼ cup *butterscotch pieces*.

Peanut Butter BEARS

It's a jungle out there, so make a few other critters to keep the bears company.

Ingredients

1 cup shortening

1 cup peanut butter

1½ cups granulated sugar

½ cup packed brown sugar

1½ teaspoons baking soda

2 eggs

1 teaspoon vanilla

2¼ cups all-purpose flour

Decorations, if you like

Utensils

Large mixing bowl

Measuring cups

Measuring spoons

Wooden spoon

Electric mixer ········

Rubber scraper

Ruler

Cookie sheet

Hot pads

Pancake turner

Wire cooling rack

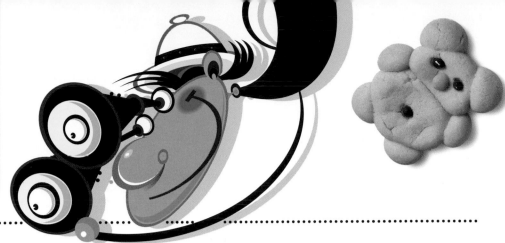

Nutrition Facts Per Cookie

Calories	247
Total fat	14 g
Saturated fat	3 g
Cholesterol	18 mg
Sodium	136 mg
Carbohydrate	27 g
Fiber	1 g
Protein	4 g

1. Turn on oven to 350°. Put shortening and peanut butter in the mixing bowl. Beat with the electric mixer on medium speed until mixed. Stop the mixer.

2. Add the granulated sugar, brown sugar, and baking soda. Beat with the electric mixer on medium speed until well mixed, stopping the mixer occasionally and scraping the bowl with the rubber scraper. Stop the mixer.

3. Add eggs and vanilla. Beat with the electric mixer on medium speed until well mixed. Stop the mixer.

4. Add the flour, ½ cup at a time, to the peanut butter mixture. Beat with the electric mixer on medium speed until well mixed. Stop the mixer; stir in any remaining flour with the wooden spoon.

5. To make one bear, shape the dough into balls of the following sizes: one 1-inch ball, one ¾-inch ball, six ½-inch balls, and one ¼-inch ball. On the ungreased cookie sheet use your hand to press gently on the 1-inch ball, flattening it to ½-inch thickness for the body. Attach the ¾-inch ball

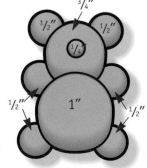

for the head; flatten it to ½-inch thickness. Attach the ½ inch balls for arms, legs, and ears. Place the ¼-inch ball on head for the nose. Repeat with remaining dough, leaving about 2 inches between bears. Or, form dough into other shapes such as bunnies, butterflies, or dinosaurs. For even baking, all cookies on cookie sheet should be about the same size.

6. Put cookie sheet in oven. Bake for 10 to 12 minutes or until cookie edges are light brown.

7. Use hot pads to remove cookie sheet from oven. Let cookies remain on cookie sheet for 1 minute. Use pancake turner to transfer cookies to the cooling rack. Repeat with remaining dough, letting cookie sheet cool between batches or using a second cookie sheet. Turn off oven.

8. When cookies are cool, decorate as you like. (If using miniature semisweet chocolate pieces for eyes and navel, press them lightly into the dough before baking the cookies.)

Peanut Butter Cookies: Roll cookie dough into 1-inch balls. Roll balls in additional granulated sugar to coat. Place on ungreased cookie sheet. Flatten the balls of dough by making crisscross marks with the tines of a fork. Bake and cool as directed above. Makes about 60 cookies.

Jumbled FRUIT Crumble

No matter how hard you try to serve this oat-topped **fruit crisp** neatly, it always ends up jumbled.

Ingredients

1   21-ounce can cherry, apple, or peach pie filling
¼   teaspoon almond extract
8   2½-inch graham cracker squares
¼   cup butter
½   cup rolled oats
¼   cup packed brown sugar
     Vanilla ice cream, if you like

Utensils

2-quart square baking dish
Can opener (if needed)
Measuring cups
Measuring spoons
Wooden spoon
Plastic bag
Rolling pin
Medium mixing bowl
Small saucepan or small microwave-safe bowl
Waxed paper (if using microwave)
Fork
Hot pads
Wire cooling rack

Nutrition Facts Per Serving	
Calories	275
Total fat	9 g
Saturated fat	5 g
Cholesterol	20 mg
Sodium	145 mg
Carbohydrate	48 g
Fiber	1 g
Protein	2 g

From
kid-tester Aaron, "This is
great! I cleaned my bowl."

1. Turn on oven to 375°. Place the pie filling and the almond extract in the ungreased baking dish. Stir gently with the wooden spoon until combined. Spread mixture evenly in the dish.

2. Put the graham crackers in the plastic bag. Seal or tie the plastic bag closed. Use the rolling pin to finely crush the crackers. (You should have about ⅔ cup crumbs.) Put crumbs in the mixing bowl. Save until Step 4.

3. Put the butter in the saucepan. Put pan on a burner. Turn burner to medium heat. Cook until butter is melted. Turn off burner. Remove pan from burner. Or, put butter in the microwave-safe bowl. Cover bowl with waxed paper. Microwave on 100% power (high) for 30 to 45 seconds or until butter is melted. Use the hot pads to remove bowl from microwave.

4. Put the melted butter, oats, and brown sugar in the bowl with the cracker crumbs. Stir mixture with the fork until combined. Sprinkle the crumb mixture over the pie filling in the dish.

5. Put baking dish in oven. Bake 20 minutes or until crumbs are lightly browned. Turn off oven. Use the hot pads to remove dish from oven. Let cool about 30 minutes on the cooling rack. Serve warm with ice cream, if you like.

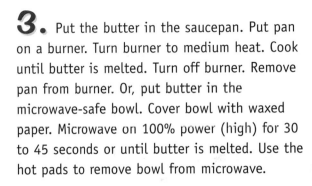

CHOCOLATE PUDDING UP CAKE

When this **crazy cake** is baked, you can have your cake and pudding, too. The cake is on the top and the fudgy pudding is on the bottom.

Ingredients

- ¹⁄₂ cup all-purpose flour
- ¹⁄₄ cup granulated sugar
- 1 tablespoon unsweetened cocoa powder
- ³⁄₄ teaspoon baking powder
- ¹⁄₄ teaspoon salt
- ¹⁄₄ cup milk
- 2 tablespoons cooking oil
- 1 teaspoon vanilla
- ¹⁄₂ cup granulated sugar
- 2 tablespoons unsweetened cocoa powder
- ³⁄₄ cup boiling water
  Whipped cream, if you like

Utensils

Measuring cups
Measuring spoons
Medium mixing bowl
Wooden spoon
1-quart casserole ⋯⋯⋯⋯
Small mixing bowl
Wooden toothpick
Hot pads
Wire cooling rack

Nutrition Facts Per Serving	
Calories	286
Total fat	8 g
Saturated fat	1 g
Cholesterol	1 mg
Sodium	211 mg
Carbohydrate	52 g
Fiber	0 g
Protein	3 g

From kid-tester Eva: "Mmm, tastes like brownies. I'll make this at home."

1. Turn on oven to 350°. Put flour, the ¼ cup sugar, the 1 tablespoon cocoa powder, baking powder, and salt in the medium mixing bowl. Use the wooden spoon to stir until well mixed.

2. Add milk, oil, and vanilla. Stir with the wooden spoon until smooth. Pour batter into the ungreased casserole.

3. Put the ½ cup sugar and the 2 tablespoons cocoa powder in the small mixing bowl. Gradually stir in the boiling water. Pour evenly over batter in casserole.

4. Put the casserole in the oven. Bake about 30 minutes or until a wooden toothpick comes out clean. (To test for doneness, use hot pads to pull out oven rack. Stick a toothpick in the center of the cake; pull out the toothpick. If any cake sticks to it, bake the cake a few minutes more and test it again.) Turn off oven. Use hot pads to remove the casserole from the oven. Set the casserole on the cooling rack to cool for 20 to 30 minutes. Serve with whipped cream, if you like.

very berry ICE

Prep: 30 minutes
Freeze: 6 hours
Makes 6 servings.

Keep cool with a scoop of this fruity frozen dessert.

Ingredients

2 cups frozen strawberries or raspberries*
1½ cups water
½ cup honey
2 tablespoons lemon juice

Utensils

Medium bowl
Sieve (if using raspberries)
Measuring cups
Measuring spoons
Electric blender
8x4x2-inch loaf pan
Foil
Ice-cream scoop or spoon

Nutrition Facts Per Serving	
Calories	103
Total fat	0 g
Saturated fat	0 g
Cholesterol	0 mg
Sodium	4 mg
Carbohydrate	27 g
Fiber	1 g
Protein	0 g

1. Partially thaw frozen berries by setting them out in the bowl at room temperature until just slightly icy (about 20 minutes); do not drain thawed berries.

2. Put berries, water, honey, and lemon juice into the blender container. Cover and blend on high speed about 1 minute or until mixture is smooth. (If you are using raspberries, you may want to strain the mixture through a sieve to remove seeds.) Pour into the loaf pan.

3. Cover pan with foil. Place pan in the freezer and freeze about 6 hours or until mixture is firm. Remove pan from freezer about 15 minutes before serving.

4. Use an ice-cream scoop or spoon to scoop or scrape ice into serving bowls.

Note: You can use fresh strawberries or raspberries, if you like. Gently rinse fresh berries in a colander and drain. Remove stems and hulls from fresh strawberries with a table knife. Continue with Step 2.

Let's Cele

Confetti Cake

Bake a **h ppy irthday** dessert that takes the cake with colorful sprinkles inside and out.

Ingredients

Shortening

1¼ cups all-purpose flour

¾ cup granulated sugar

1¼ teaspoons baking powder

¼ teaspoon salt

¾ cup milk

⅓ cup butter or margarine, softened

1 teaspoon vanilla

1 egg

2 tablespoons small, multicolored decorative candies

Vanilla or chocolate frosting, if you like

Utensils

8x8x2-inch baking pan

Large mixing bowl

Measuring cups

Measuring spoons

Electric mixer ·········

Rubber scraper

Wooden spoon

Hot pads

Wooden toothpick

Wire cooling rack

Nutrition Facts Per Serving (without frosting)

Calories	230
Total fat	9 g
Saturated fat	5 g
Cholesterol	49 mg
Sodium	221 mg
Carbohydrate	35 g
Fiber	0 g
Protein	3 g

1. Turn on oven to 375°. Grease the bottom of the baking pan with shortening. Save until Step 5.

2. Put flour, sugar, baking powder, and salt in the mixing bowl. Add milk, butter or margarine, and vanilla to the dry ingredients.

3. Beat with the electric mixer on low speed until ingredients are combined. Stop mixer and scrape sides of bowl with the rubber scraper. Beat on medium speed for 2 minutes more. Turn off mixer.

4. Add egg. Beat on low speed until combined, then beat on medium speed for 2 minutes more.

5. Use the wooden spoon to stir in the decorative candies. Pour batter into the prepared baking pan, scraping bowl with rubber scraper to remove all the batter. Spread batter evenly in pan.

6. Put pan in oven. Bake 25 to 30 minutes or until a wooden toothpick comes out clean. (To test for doneness, use hot pads to pull out oven rack. Stick a toothpick in the center of the cake; pull out the toothpick. If any cake sticks to it, bake the cake a few minutes more and test it again.) Turn off oven. Use hot pads to remove pan from oven. Set pan on cooling rack. Cool cake completely. Spread with frosting, if you like.

Eat your Heart OUT COOKIES

Don't wait until Valentine's Day to share these heartwarming chocolate cookies.

Ingredients

Butter or margarine
1 cup semisweet chocolate pieces
¼ cup light-colored corn syrup
2 tablespoons butter or margarine
3 cups crisp rice cereal
Frosting, if you like

Utensils

Cookie sheet
Waxed paper
Heavy medium saucepan or 1½-quart microwave-safe casserole
Measuring cups
Measuring spoons
Wooden spoon
Ruler
Heart-shaped cookie cutter
Plastic wrap

Nutrition Facts Per Serving (without frosting)

Calories	193
Total fat	9 g
Saturated fat	2 g
Cholesterol	8 mg
Sodium	147 mg
Carbohydrate	31 g
Fiber	0 g
Protein	2 g

From kid-tester Melissa: "This is my favorite recipe. It's easy and fast to make."

1. Line the cookie sheet with waxed paper. Grease the waxed paper with butter or margarine. Save until Step 4.

2. Put the chocolate pieces, corn syrup, and the 2 tablespoons butter or margarine in the saucepan. Put pan on burner. Turn burner to low heat. Cook until chocolate and butter are melted, stirring all the time with the wooden spoon. Turn off burner. Remove pan from burner. Or, put chocolate pieces, corn syrup, and butter or margarine in the microwave-safe casserole. Microwave, uncovered, on 100% power (high) for 1 minute or until chocolate and butter are melted, stirring once.

3. Add the rice cereal to the melted chocolate mixture. Stir with the wooden spoon until the cereal is evenly coated with chocolate.

4. Turn the chocolate-coated cereal out onto the prepared cookie sheet. Pat it into a 12×6-inch rectangle. Chill about 20 minutes or until slightly firm.

5. Cut cereal mixture into heart shapes with the cookie cutter. Decorate with frosting, if you like. Chill until firm; wrap each heart in plastic wrap. Chill until serving time.

C
E
L
E
B
R
A
T
E

Hangin' Out COOKIES

Cookies that look as good as they taste can double as holiday decorations.

Ingredients

- ½ cup butter or margarine
- 1 cup granulated sugar
- 2 teaspoons baking powder
- ½ teaspoon ground nutmeg, if you like
- 1 egg
- 2 tablespoons milk
- ½ teaspoon vanilla
- 2¼ cups all-purpose flour

  Assorted decorations (colored sugar; small, multicolored decorative candies; and/or crushed hard candies)

  Canned creamy white frosting (tinted to desired colors)

  Narrow ribbon

Utensils

Table knife
Measuring cups
Measuring spoons
Large mixing bowl
Electric mixer ....
Rubber scraper
Wooden spoon
Rolling pin
Assorted cookie cutters or knife
Cookie sheet
Plastic drinking straw
Hot pads
Pancake turner
Wire cooling rack
Wooden toothpick
Small bowls

Nutrition Facts Per Cookie (without frosting)	
Calories	87
Total fat	3 g
Saturated fat	2 g
Cholesterol	15 mg
Sodium	58 mg
Carbohydrate	13 g
Fiber	0 g
Protein	1 g

1. Turn on oven to 375°. Cut up the butter or margarine with the table knife.

2. Put butter or margarine in the mixing bowl. Beat with the electric mixer on medium speed about 30 seconds or until butter is softened. Stop mixer. Add the sugar, baking powder, and, nutmeg, if you like. Beat on medium speed until combined, stopping the mixer occasionally and scraping the bowl with the rubber scraper. Stop mixer.

3. Add the egg, milk, and vanilla. Beat on medium speed until combined. Beat in as much of the flour as you can with the mixer. Stop mixer. Stir in any remaining flour with the wooden spoon. (If the dough is soft, wrap it in plastic wrap and chill about 1 hour.)

4. Divide dough in half. On a lightly floured surface, use the rolling pin to roll out a portion of dough to about ¼-inch thickness. Cut into desired shapes with cookie cutters or knife, rerolling dough as necessary. If dough begins to soften, put it in the refrigerator to chill. Transfer cookies to ungreased cookie sheet, leaving about

2 inches between cookies. With the plastic drinking straw, make a hole at top of each cookie.

5. Put cookie sheet in oven. Bake for 8 to 10 minutes or until the cookie edges are light brown.

6. Use the hot pads to remove cookie sheet from oven. While cookies are hot, if necessary, reopen holes with the toothpick. Use the pancake turner to transfer cookies to the cooling rack. Repeat with remaining dough. Turn off oven.

7. When cookies are cool, put assorted decorations in small plastic bowls. Attach decorations to the cookies with some frosting, using the table knife to spread the frosting. Thread a small piece of ribbon through the hole in each cookie. Tie ribbon for hanging.

8. Let cookies stand about 30 minutes or until frosting is slightly dry.

Celebration COOKIE PIZZA

Prep: 20 minutes
Bake: 12 minutes
Makes 12 servings.

For another **party dessert** idea, spread the cooled cookie crust with canned chocolate or vanilla frosting in place of the pudding. Sprinkle it with your favorite candy pieces.

Ingredients

- 1 18-ounce roll refrigerated chocolate chip or sugar cookie dough

- 2 3½- to 5-ounce containers chocolate or vanilla pudding (about ⅔ to ¾ cup total)

- ½ cup plain yogurt

- ⅓ cup peanut butter

- 2 medium bananas, sliced, and/or ½ cup miniature semisweet chocolate pieces or chopped peanuts

Utensils

12-inch pizza pan
Hot pads
Wire cooling rack
Measuring cups
Small mixing bowl
Rubber scraper
Sharp knife

Nutrition Facts Per Serving

Calories	277
Total fat	13 g
Saturated fat	5 g
Cholesterol	14 mg
Sodium	205 mg
Carbohydrate	37 g
Fiber	2 g
Protein	4 g

1. Turn on oven to 350°. Using your fingers, press the cookie dough evenly into the ungreased pizza pan.* If you need to keep the dough from sticking, dip your fingers into a little flour first.

2. Place pan in oven. Bake for 12 to 15 minutes or until cookie dough is golden. Turn off oven. Remove pan from oven with hot pads and place on the cooling rack. Let cookie crust cool completely. Save until Step 4.

3. Put the pudding, yogurt, and peanut butter in the mixing bowl. Stir together with the rubber scraper.

4. Use the rubber scraper to spread the mixture evenly over the cookie crust. Top with bananas and/or chocolate pieces or peanuts.

5. Cut into wedges with the sharp knife and serve immediately.

Note: If you want to take the whole cookie crust out of the pan to serve, line the pizza pan with foil before pressing the cookie dough into the pan.

FANTASTIC FUDGE

Prep: 20 minutes
Chill: several hours
Makes 64 pieces.

When you want a special little sweet to eat, just fudge it!

Ingredients

Butter or margarine, softened

1 1-pound package powdered sugar

$\frac{1}{2}$ cup unsweetened cocoa powder

$\frac{1}{2}$ cup nonfat dry milk powder

$\frac{1}{3}$ cup water

$\frac{1}{2}$ cup butter or margarine

$\frac{1}{2}$ cup chopped nuts, if you like

Utensils

8x8x2-inch baking pan

Foil

Large mixing bowl

Measuring cups

Small saucepan or 1-quart microwave-safe casserole

Waxed paper (if using microwave)

Wooden spoon

Ruler

Table knife

Sharp knife

Nutrition Facts Per Piece

Calories	51
Total fat	2 g
Saturated fat	1 g
Cholesterol	4 mg
Sodium	18 mg
Carbohydrate	8 g
Fiber	0 g
Protein	1 g

Kid-tester Austin
loved the fudge.
"It's so-o-o-o nice and rich."

1. Line the baking pan with foil, letting the foil hang over the pan's edges. Grease foil with butter or margarine. Save until Step 5.

2. Stir powdered sugar and cocoa powder together in the large mixing bowl. Save until Step 4.

3. Stir together the dry milk powder and water in a small saucepan until powder is dissolved. Add the ½ cup butter or margarine. Put pan on a burner. Turn burner to medium heat. Cook just until mixture boils, using the wooden spoon to stir all the time to melt the butter or margarine. Turn off burner. Remove pan from burner. Or, put the butter or margarine in the microwave-safe casserole. Cover casserole with waxed paper. Microwave on 100% power (high) about 1 minute or until butter is melted. Stir in the dry milk powder and water with the wooden spoon. Microwave, uncovered, for 1 to 2 minutes more or until mixture just begins to boil, stirring twice with the wooden spoon.

4. Pour the melted butter mixture into the powdered sugar mixture in the mixing bowl. Stir with the wooden spoon until smooth. Add the chopped nuts, if you like, and stir with the wooden spoon until combined.

5. Pour fudge into the prepared pan, spreading it evenly. While fudge is still warm, use the table knife and ruler to mark the surface with 1-inch squares. Chill several hours or until fudge is firm.

6. When fudge is firm, use the foil to lift it out of the pan. Using the sharp knife, cut fudge into squares. Or, cut into shapes with cookie cutters. Store tightly covered in the refrigerator.

C E L E B R A T E

PARENTS

Cooking
with kids

What is it about a kitchen that attracts a crowd? Maybe it's that so much happens there during the preparation of meals. And kids love being part of it all, so it's the perfect opportunity for you and your children to have some fun together.

You're the best teacher your children can have in the kitchen. And learning about food—what foods we should eat, how to choose foods for a balanced diet, planning meals, how to read a recipe, kitchen safety—results in skills that last a lifetime.

In addition to teaching important food information and food preparation skills, cooking helps kids improve their reading and math comprehension, their hand-eye coordination, their ability to follow directions and make observations, and their creativity. It also encourages their natural curiosity about how things work.

Cooking with children is all about teamwork. As you work with them in the kitchen, you'll find that their abilities and confidence levels grow. They'll enjoy being able to spend time with you and share the excitement of watching their creations take shape.

Getting kids to eat right

Teaching kids how to eat right starts at the beginning with the raw ingredients. Encourage your children to come along and explore the market or grocery store with you, identifying foods they know and like, asking about unfamiliar foods, and selecting foods they would like to help prepare. Kids often prefer to eat what they have had a hand in making.

One of the simplest ways to ensure your children won't turn their noses up at what you put on the table is to set a good example. Eat a variety of foods yourself and don't be obvious about your dislikes. Seeing you eat a certain food might pique their interest enough for them to try it and like it as well.

Like adults, kids enjoy foods that look appealing. Although many younger kids prefer plain, less spicy foods, they still desire interesting shapes, textures, colors, and imaginative descriptions of what's on their plates. But no matter how hard you try, every food cannot be a winner. Like you, your kids will have preferences, so encourage them to try everything—to have a new food experience as often as possible. Then respect their right to say, "No thanks, I really don't care for that." At least they've tried it.

As they grow, children's preferences change, sometimes quickly, so don't be discouraged. It's what they eat over several days that matters— not what they eat on a particular day.

How to use this cookbook

● Start your aspiring chefs off right by reviewing the information in "Start With the Basics" (beginning on page 4). The chapter highlights some preliminary cooking information, such as how to read recipes and measure ingredients. You'll also find notes on nutrition.

● The recipes in this book appeal to a variety of skill levels. Help your children pick recipes that match their abilities—and their taste buds.

● Supervise your children in the kitchen according to their experience. Some kids may be perfectly comfortable using a stove but need an assistant when using a sharp knife.

● Establish guidelines about what utensils and appliances are off-limits when you're not around.

● Insist on proper kitchen and food safety—well-washed hands are a must!

● **Have fun** and enjoy the time you spend with your kids at mealtimes.

Sensible snacking

Make snacks work for you—not against you. A planned snack at least a couple of hours before a meal can be used to fill in gaps in your child's nutrition, without ruining his or her appetite. In fact, two or three snacks a day help supply the energy growing children need; maintaining a snack schedule prevents inappropriate eating between meals.

Make sure the snacks, like meals, are healthy. Keep some better-for-you selections on hand, such as pretzels, rice cakes, low-fat crackers, flour tortillas, popcorn, cut-up vegetables, fresh or canned fruit (in natural juice), cheese, yogurt, hard-cooked eggs, and fruit juices.

Avoid labeling foods such as candy or pop "bad." This label practically guarantees they'll be appealing to kids. Teach your children how to incorporate these foods into their diets occasionally so they learn how to handle them appropriately. Remember, everything in moderation is a wise rule.

Craft RECIPES

When you're in need of a new playtime activity for your kids, try one of these homemade recipes for fun.

Bubbles

- ¼ **cup liquid detergent (preferably Dawn)**
- ½ **cup water**
- 1 **teaspoon sugar or 3 tablespoons glycerine (can be purchased at most pharmacies)**

Mix all ingredients in a flat container such as a dishpan or baking pan.

Dip purchased bubble wands or homemade bubble blowers into the mixture, then wave the wands slowly in the air.

You can turn household items into bubble blowers easily. For example, poke the bottom out of a paper cup or try a slotted spoon, a plastic berry basket, or a drinking straw.

Glob

- 4 **ounces white school glue**
- 1 **cup water**
   Few drops liquid food coloring
- 1 **teaspoon Borax**

In a bowl stir together glue and ½ cup of the water. Add food coloring.

In another bowl stir together the remaining ½ cup water and Borax.

Stir the Borax mixture into glue mixture. You should have a thick mass in a liquid. When the Glob has formed into a solid mass, pour off the remaining liquid and discard it. Glob thickens when you knead, stretch, and play with it.

CAUTION: Do not eat. May stain clothes, carpet, and furniture.

Finger Paint

In a large saucepan combine 1 cup *all-purpose flour* and 1 cup *cold water*. Stir until smooth. Add 3 cups additional cold water. Cook and stir over medium heat until mixture thickens and bubbles. Reduce heat. Cook and stir 1 minute more. Remove pan from heat. Pour mixture into 3 heatproof bowls. Use *food coloring* to tint the paint the desired colors. Cover each bowl with plastic wrap. Let paint stand at room temperature until cool.

Modeling Clay

1 **cup cornstarch**
1 **16-ounce box baking soda**
1½ **cups water**

In a large saucepan combine cornstarch and baking soda. Stir in water. Cook and stir over low heat until mixture thickens and forms a ball. Remove pan from heat.

Dust work surface lightly with cornstarch. Turn clay out onto surface. When it's cool enough to handle, knead clay until smooth.

Place clay in a bowl. Cover bowl with plastic wrap; cool completely. (If desired, tightly wrap clay and refrigerate up to 2 weeks. When ready to use, knead to soften.)

Use clay to make various shapes. For holiday ornaments, roll dough to ¼-inch thickness. Cut out shapes with cookie cutters.

Allow the clay to air-dry. Or, for bigger pieces, place shapes on a baking sheet and bake in a 300° oven for 30 minutes. Turn off the oven; leave baking sheet in oven 1 hour more. If the clay is still not dry, place it on a wire cooling rack and let it air-dry. (Baked clay will acquire a slight brownness during baking.)

When dry, use paints to decorate the shapes.

Clay Dough

3 **cups all-purpose flour**
1 **cup salt**
2 **tablespoons cornstarch**
1¼ **cups water**
2 **teaspoons cooking oil**
  Food coloring

In a large mixing bowl combine flour, salt, and cornstarch. In a small mixing bowl combine water and cooking oil. Gradually stir water mixture into dry ingredients until combined. Knead until smooth.

Divide dough into portions and knead in food coloring. (Add small amounts of water if dough is dry; add small amounts of flour if dough is sticky.) Keep any unused dough wrapped in plastic wrap to prevent drying.

Use clay dough to make various shapes. To dry shapes, let them stand until firm, turning occasionally; it will take several days.

Index

Metric Cooking Hints

By making a few conversions, cooks in Australia, Canada, and the United Kingdom can use the recipes in *Better Homes and Gardens® New Junior Cookbook* with confidence. The charts on this page provide a guide for converting measurements from the U.S. customary system, which is used throughout this book, to the imperial and metric systems. There also is a conversion table for oven temperatures to accommodate the differences in oven calibrations.

Product Differences: Most of the ingredients called for in the recipes in this book are available in English-speaking countries. However, some are known by different names. Here are some common American ingredients and their possible counterparts:

● Sugar is granulated or castor sugar.
● Powdered sugar is icing sugar.
● All-purpose flour is plain household flour or white flour. When self-rising flour is used in place of all-purpose flour in a recipe that calls for leavening, omit the leavening agent (baking soda or baking powder) and salt.
● Light-colored corn syrup is golden syrup.
● Cornstarch is cornflour.
● Baking soda is bicarbonate of soda.
● Vanilla is vanilla essence.
● Green, red, or yellow sweet peppers are capsicums.

Volume and Weight: Americans traditionally use cup measures for liquid and solid ingredients. The chart, *top right,* shows the approximate imperial and metric equivalents. If you are accustomed to weighing solid ingredients, the following approximate equivalents will be helpful.

● 1 cup butter, castor sugar, or rice = 8 ounces = about 250 grams
● 1 cup flour = 4 ounces = about 125 grams
● 1 cup icing sugar = 5 ounces = about 150 grams

Spoon measures are used for smaller amounts of ingredients. Although the size of the tablespoon varies slightly in different countries, for practical purposes and for recipes in this book, a straight substitution is all that's necessary.

Measurements made using cups or spoons always should be level unless stated otherwise.

Equivalents: U.S. = Australia/U.K.

⅛ teaspoon = 0.5 millilitre
¼ teaspoon = 1 millilitre
½ teaspoon = 2 millilitre
1 teaspoon = 5 millilitre
1 tablespoon = 15 millilitre
¼ cup = 2 fluid ounces = 60 millilitre
⅓ cup = 3 fluid ounces = 90 millilitre
½ cup = 4 fluid ounces = 120 millilitre
⅔ cup = 5 fluid ounces = 150 millilitre
¾ cup = 6 fluid ounces = 180 millilitre
1 cup = 8 fluid ounces = 240 millilitre
2 cups = 16 fluid ounces (1 pint) = 475 millilitre
1 quart = 32 fluid ounces (2 pints) = 1 litre
½ inch = 1.27 centimetre
1 inch = 2.54 centimetre

Baking Pan Sizes

American	Metric
8×1½-inch round baking pan	20×4-centimetre cake tin
9×1½-inch round baking pan	23×3.5-centimetre cake tin
11×7×1½-inch baking pan	28×18×4-centimetre baking tin
13×9×2-inch baking pan	30×20×3-centimetre baking tin
2-quart rectangular baking dish	30×20×3-centimetre baking tin
15×10×1-inch baking pan	30×25×2-centimetre baking tin (Swiss roll tin)
9-inch pie plate	22×4- or 23×4-centimetre pie plate
7- or 8-inch springform pan	18- or 20-centimetre springform or loose-bottom cake tin
9×5×3-inch loaf pan	23×13×7-centimetre or 2-pound narrow loaf tin or paté tin
1½-quart casserole	1.5-litre casserole
2-quart casserole	2-litre casserole

Oven Temperature Equivalents

Fahrenheit Setting	Celsius Setting*	Gas Setting
300°F	150°C	Gas Mark 2 (slow)
325°F	160°C	Gas Mark 3 (moderately slow)
350°F	180°C	Gas Mark 4 (moderate)
375°F	190°C	Gas Mark 5 (moderately hot)
400°F	200°C	Gas Mark 6 (hot)
425°F	220°C	Gas Mark 7
450°F	230°C	Gas Mark 8 (very hot)
Broil		Grill

*Electric and gas ovens may be calibrated using Celsius. However, for an electric oven, increase the Celsius setting 10° to 20° when cooking above 160°C. For convection or forced-air ovens (gas or electric), lower the temperature setting 10°C when cooking at all heat levels.